THE **STUPID**
CROOK BOOK

Leland Gregory

**Andrews McMeel
Publishing**
Kansas City

02 03 04 05 06 EBI 10 9 8 7 6 5 4 3 2

ISBN: 0-7407-2694-3

Library of Congress Control Number: 2002102324

Book design by Holly Camerlinck

Attention: Schools and Businesses
Andrews McMeel books are available at quantity discounts with bulk purchase
for educational, business, or sales promotional use. For information, please write
to: Special Sales Department, Andrews McMeel Publishing, 4520 Main Street,
Kansas City, Missouri 64111.

This book is dedicated to my wife and partner in crime, Gloria Graves Gregory. I love you and I'm honored to be spending my life with you.

Introduction

First let me say that I know that to be grammatically correct this book should be titled *The Book of Stupid Crooks*. But honestly, a book about bumbling burglars, dim-witted robbers, dumb pickpockets, intellectually challenged confidence men, boneheaded bank robbers, and thickheaded thieves doesn't really warrant it; and besides, *The Stupid Crook Book* is funnier. In most cases I've altered or eliminated the names of the suspects or criminals because, even though in most cases they're extremely stupid, they still have the ability to hire lawyers. In every instance, however, the facts are true and have been taken strictly from legitimate news sources (there are no Siamese-twin criminals who have lost 150 pounds on the alien-Bigfoot diet). I would like to extend my undying gratitude to the men and women of law enforcement who put their lives on the line every day to keep us safe and who are forced to wade into the shallow end of the gene pool when dealing with the type of dummies included in this book.

THIS GAS TASTES FUNNY!

*L*arceny is defined as the taking and removing of another person's personal property. The property in question is usually valuable, but in the case of one Seattle, Washington, man the stolen property was just plain crap. Police arrived on the scene at a recreational vehicle park to discover a very sick man vomiting and complaining of stomach cramps. The man admitted he had attempted to siphon gas from a motor home but had inadvertently put the siphon tube into the wrong tank. Instead of gasoline the man had sucked out the contents of the sewage holding tank. The owner declined to press charges, as he was too busy laughing.

"This is a bank robbery of the Federal Reserve Bank
of Dallas, Texas. Give me all the money.
Thank you, Ronnie Darnell Bell."

Note found on alleged intended bank robber Ronnie Darnell Bell.

TWO DUMBBELLS

The alarm sounded at the Buffum-Downtown YMCA in Long Beach, California, and the police arrived within five minutes. They soon discovered two men trying to steal six forty-five-pound barbells that were loaded into a rickety shopping cart. Too bad the two thieves were two ninety-five-pound weaklings, because the shopping cart kept tipping over on them as they tried to escape. "They weren't even very big guys," said Tim Hardy, physical education director at the gym. When the police cornered them, the two thieves struggled to lift the barbells into a trash bin. They were quickly arrested and placed on $5,000 bond each. There was no explanation why the two dumbbells wanted the six barbells–they were only worth about sixty cents a pound. Maybe they knew they would eventually be arrested and wanted to tone up before going to prison.

IT'S NOT POLITE TO POINT

We all know the scene in the movies where the would-be robber sticks his finger in his pocket and pretends it's a gun, right? Well, apparently one robber thought that was a good idea and tried it out in an attempt to rob a Bank of America in Merced, California. But he forgot one thing–he forgot to hide his finger in his pocket. The index-indicating idiot pointed his uncovered finger, with his thumb cocked, of course, at the teller, demanding money. The teller asked the robber to wait, then walked away. After some time the bank robber got tired of waiting. He unloaded his finger, walked out of the bank, and went across the street to another bank. This time he tried a different approach. He leaped over the counter and tried to wrestle the cash-drawer key from a teller. An employee grabbed the key and told the thwarted thief to "get out of there," according to Sergeant Gary Austin. The two-time loser was arrested shortly thereafter when he was discovered sitting in a clump of nearby shrubs. I guess now every time he sticks his finger up his nose it can be considered a suicide attempt.

SAVE ME FROM MYSELF

*M*ost of the stories in this book show how one, or maybe two, very stupid actions can result in the arrest of a criminal. But one Pittsburgh, Pennsylvania, criminal (whom I'll lovingly refer to as Our Crook) holds the record for moronic moves–eight to be exact. Here they are, in chronological order, a clumsy criminal's attempts to break into a shed, a garage, and a home.

Moronic Move Number One: Our Crook smashes his fist through a window in the shed–shredding his hand.

Moronic Move Number Two: Our Crook successfully breaks into the second story of the nearby garage. The garage is dark; Our Crook doesn't have a flashlight, doesn't see the hole in the floor, falls through it, and winds up bruised, dazed, and confused on the first floor.

Moronic Move Number Three: While staggering around on the first floor of the garage, our bewildered burglar falls into the grease pit–cracking his cranium.

Moronic Move Number Four: The garage has gotten the best of Our Crook, so he decides to break into the house. He shatters the window in the front door, creeps inside, and promptly tumbles down the cellar stairs.

Moronic Move Number Five: Our Crook finally realizes this isn't his day. He leaves the house and gets into his car. He drives downhill, loses control of the car, and hits a tree. His already damaged head (see Moronic Move Number Three) strikes the steering wheel with great force.

Moronic Move Number Six: Not wanting any criminal element to get away with his getaway car, Our Crook gets out of his car and locks all the doors. For some reason he then retraces his steps to the garage and retraces his fall into the grease pit.

Moronic Move Number Seven: Our Crook staggers out of the garage and decides to go back home. He reaches into his pocket to retrieve his car keys but can't find them. He smashes his car's rear window, climbs in over the backseat, and breaks the gearshift getting the car into neutral. As the car begins rolling down the hill, Our Crook pops the clutch to jump-start the car–and he succeeds, but he can't unlock the steering wheel. He crashes into a second tree.

Moronic Move Number Eight: The third blow to his head causes Our Crook to lose consciousness. His noggin falls against the steering wheel, setting off the car horn. The blaring horn alerts the neighbors, who call the cops, who arrest Our Crook. He pleads guilty to a charge of criminal mischief (he never actually stole anything) and is christened the Bad-Luck Burglar by the police.

I don't know about you, but I feel humbled in the presence of such overwhelming stupidity.

A MIND IS A TERRIBLE THING TO READ

You're in the middle of a home robbery. You've just discovered a diamond ring but you're wondering where the other "good" stuff could be hidden. What do you do? Well, one burglar who found himself in such a predicament picked up the phone and dialed a psychic hot line. The thief didn't just have a quick chat with the psychic; he stayed on the line long enough to total $250 in charges. How was our nonclairvoyant criminal apprehended? While chatting away with the psychic, he used his real name. When the phone bill came in later that month, the homeowners saw the outrageous 900-number call and called the police, who traced it back to the psychic. Even though the crook was dumb enough to use his real name, a truly gifted psychic, in my opinion, should have known who he was anyway.

According to the FBI, the average number of bank robbers who are arrested each year because they were stupid enough to write their holdup notes on the backs of their own deposit slips: forty-five.

DELI DOS AND DON'TS

*N*atron Fubble quickly entered a Miami delicatessen and placed his order. Instead of asking for a nice egg-salad sandwich, Fubble asked for all the money in the cash register. And instead of giving him the cold, hard cash, the owner smashed him in the face with a cold, hard salami. Fubble fumbled out of the delicatessen and hid himself and his pulsating proboscis in the trunk of a parked car. Unknown to Fubble, he had chosen as his hideaway the trunk of an undercover police team who were staked out observing another criminal's activities. Police officers finally heard Fubble's moaning and his attempts to breathe through his salami-snapped septum. But they didn't discover him immediately; you see, the officers weren't in the car at the time of Fubble's arrival . . . and didn't return to it for five days. Being locked in a trunk for five days, it's probably a good thing Fubble's nose *was* out of commission.

TRAFFIC JAM

*T*hings were going smoothly for a burglar as he broke into the Hill-Rom Corporation in Pennsauken, New Jersey. He had opened the door and, as he had seen hundreds of times in the movies, knew exactly how to keep the lock from latching behind him. He removed a piece of paper from his pocket, folded it, and carefully placed the paper between the latch and the door frame, ensuring that the door wouldn't lock while he was scampering about inside, cleaning out the place. His deed done, he left through the door he had ingeniously rigged and made his escape. When the police arrived to investigate the robbery, they noticed a folded piece of paper by the doorjamb. They opened it and the case was solved. It wasn't a confession–it was a traffic ticket. The ticket, complete with home address and telephone number, had been issued to the burglar the night before, citing him for driving with a cracked windshield. He was promptly arrested and all the stolen property was recovered. A cracked windshield, huh? Sounds like a pretty good description of the suspect, doesn't it?

In Wellington, New Zealand, a young man held a radio-station manager hostage, locked the both of them in the studio, and forced him to play the song "The Rainbow Connection" by Kermit the Frog.

IT'S DÉJÀ VU ALL OVER AGAIN

*I*f at first you don't succeed, try, try again" must have been running through the mind of this story's repeat offender sometime during his short criminal career. The Troy, Alabama, man was arrested and pleaded guilty to breaking into the Deja Vu store–twice. Our recidivist, who apparently wasn't very original, smashed the same window and stole much of the same merchandise. He was arrested because the same witness identified him both times. I wonder if he'll get off because of the rule of double jeopardy?

A survey published in Whittle Communications' SPECIAL REPORT magazine revealed that 27 percent of home burglars like to raid the refrigerator while on the job.

TAKE A HIKE

*T*he clerk stood terrified as the knife-wielding robber loomed in front of him. He did just as he was asked, turning over everything in the cash register, all of sixty-nine dollars. But the thief wanted more. On his way out he confiscated a pair of tan hiking boots, then hit the getaway trail. The accused robber was apprehended and held over for trial. During the proceedings the clerk positively identified the defendant as the man who perpetrated the robbery—but other than an identification, the prosecuting attorney had little evidence to convict. That's when the defendant started feeling confident about getting released and propped his feet up on the table. "I leaned over and stared," said Judge James Fleetwood. "I said, 'Surely nobody would be so stupid as to wear the boots he stole to his trial.'" The clerk quickly identified the tan hiking boots on the defendant's feet as the ones lifted from his store. The jury barely turned on their heels before they found him guilty of aggravated robbery. He was taken away and his boots were confiscated. "We sent him back to jail in his stocking feet," Fleetwood added. If they always remove stolen items from your person before they send you to jail, it's a good thing the guy hadn't stolen a pair of pants and underwear.

A TURN FOR THE WORSE

A patrolman in Suffield, Connecticut, spotted a speeding car and began pursuit. The officer was informed that the vehicle matched the description of one used in the robbery of a bakery seven miles north of town. The driver looked in the rearview mirror and quickly realized he was being chased. He thought he would outsmart the cops–but you've got to have smarts to do that. He pulled into a spacious parking lot, jumped out of his car, and ran into the front lobby of a large building to hide. He was surprised, however, when the doors closed behind him and locked. "I believe he thought it was a mall," said Patrolman Michael Lewandowski. "But I've never seen too many malls with razor wire across the top." The fast-driving but slow-thinking criminal had pulled into the parking lot of MacDougall Correctional Institution, a high-security prison. He was charged with several motor vehicle offenses and with being a fugitive from justice. And some people claim men are bad with directions–this guy knew where he was headed all along.

THE BONG SHOW

A woman in Southborough, Massachusetts, accidentally dialed 911 instead of directory assistance, 411, then quickly hung up when she heard the emergency dispatcher. She didn't think anything about her misdialing until a few minutes later, when two police officers knocked at her door. The woman tried to dismiss the officers and they became suspicious because she was acting so—well, suspicious. The officer and his partner convinced the woman to let them look around and make sure everything was all right. She looked at her husband, he nodded, and they let the officers in. The officers walked through the house and didn't notice anything unusual, until they saw the woman trying to hide a cigar box and a bong. According to the officers, the cigar box contained only a small amount of marijuana—but after a few questions by the police, the woman and her husband showed the officers where the rest of their stash was hidden. They were arrested. And people still wonder why they call it dope.

A woman in Elgin, Texas, was arrested and charged with shoplifting. The woman was seen taking an item off the shelf, walking around the store devouring the contents, and then leaving without paying for it. She was charged with stealing a jar of pickled pigs' feet.

SPACE CADETS

What's taking so long?" thought one of the two robbers of a local grocery store in Larch Barrens, Maryland. The dim-witted duo thought the laser they had stolen earlier would cut through the store's safe like it was butter. Maybe they had the setting wrong. Maybe the safe was stronger than they thought. Or maybe they were just stupid. When the police arrived, the two were still hunched over the safe, trying to cut through to the money hidden inside. The police confiscated the laser, and the two admitted they had stolen it from a local amusement center earlier in the day. It was a Lazer Tag gun, a battery-operated toy, and the two had been shining its harmless light on the safe for nearly an hour before the police arrived. Beam me up, Scotty. There's no sign of intelligent life on this planet.

The timing was off for a bank robber in Cheshire, Massachusetts. He pulled off the heist at 4:30 P.M. and tried to make his getaway through downtown North Adams. Stuck in rush-hour traffic, he was apprehended by an officer on foot.

DOG-DAY AFTERNOON

*I*mages of a feast with sirloins and ribs, T-bone steaks, filet mignon, veal, roasts, and other delicacies must have crossed the minds of the thieves when they broke into a commercial freezer and stole nine bundles wrapped in black plastic. As they loaded up their car, they probably discussed what would be good side items: baked potatoes, a garden salad with vinaigrette dressing, Jell-O? Their mouths were watering, and they couldn't wait to get home and fire up the grill. They lost their appetites, I'm sure, when they unwrapped the packages and discovered the frozen bodies of dogs, cats, and a ferret or two. Apparently the crooks didn't notice that the freezer was located behind the Paradise Valley Road Pet Hospital. There could be a new advertising slogan in all this: "Fido, the other white meat!"

LET YOUR FINGERS DO THE WALKING

A twenty-four-year-old migrant fruit picker from Quebec was helping himself to a tank full of someone else's gas, courtesy of a siphon hose. After he drained the contents, he realized the hose had gotten stuck in the tank, so he poked his little finger inside the tank opening to free the hose. Bad move. Now both the hose and his little finger were trapped, because a spring-loaded flap inside the gas tank had clamped down on them. His accomplices couldn't get his finger out, so they did the next best thing–they ran away. Not wanting their friend to stay stuck red-handed–or red-fingered–they decided that the noble thing would be to call 911 and turn him in. An ambulance was the first on the scene, but the paramedics couldn't get the man's finger out of the tank. The police arrived soon after, but they couldn't get the finger out either. Finally firefighters moved the van, with the crook still stuck, onto the street to give them more room to cut off a portion of the gas tank. The man, his finger, and the pipe were all taken to a local hospital, where doctors were finally able to extract his trapped pinkie. His pinkie was free now, but he wasn't–he was taken to jail and eventually sentenced to time served, eight months of probation, and twenty hours of community service and ordered to pay $500 to get the van repaired. After the man was sentenced, I wonder if he thought about giving his friends who'd fingered him the finger.

THAT'S A LITTLE MORE INFORMATION THAN WE NEEDED

A man in Las Vegas was reading in the local paper about a suspect who was wanted on charges of several sexual assaults in the area–and to his surprise, he noticed a striking resemblance between himself and the wanted man. It wasn't him, of course, but he wanted the authorities to know that he wasn't the one they were looking for. When he dropped by the station, police assured the paranoid man that he wasn't a suspect in the case and thanked him for doing his civic duty. On a hunch, the police then ran the man's name through their computer and soon arrested him on an outstanding warrant from California for assault and drug charges. Hey, the guy must have thought to himself, "I may be a violent drug addict, but I'm not a rapist."

WELL, HE WAS UNDER OATH

A man convicted of robbery asked the Texas Court of Appeals to overrule his guilty verdict on the basis of a self-incriminating answer given at his trial. During a break in the trial, there was concern that the suspect had fraternized with some witnesses who were to take the stand against him. The judge asked the suspect to tell him exactly which witnesses he had contacted, and the man answered, "The ones that I robbed."

Seventy-five dollars was stolen from a Chicago man by a robber using a manhole cover as a weapon.

A ROBBERY THAT WAS IN THE BAG

To pull off a successful bank robbery you not only need to have a well-thought-out plan, you must also accomplish the listed items on the plan in order. It was the last part in Bank Robbery 101 that this Charlotte, North Carolina, man didn't grasp. He remembered the gun; he remembered the getaway car; he even remembered to wear a disguise. As disguises go, however, it wasn't the most original–a simple paper bag with eyeholes cut out. The problem wasn't with having the mask, it was when he decided to put it over his head–while he was driving the car and still blocks from the bank. Several drivers noticed the "unknown driver" and called police about the suspicious man wearing a bag over his head. The robber pulled up to the bank, got out of his car, and walked straight to a teller to make his demands. The teller had a hard time understanding the bagged bad guy because he had forgotten to cut a mouth hole in the bag. Finally, he made himself understood, got his hands on a fistful of money, and ran out of the bank. Of course by this time the man's plans had been let out of the bag by the numerous calls to the police, and he was arrested immediately after he exited the bank.

CRIMINAL ON DISPLAY

*T*ellers at a branch of the Bank of New Hampshire in Littleton were suspicious of a man they saw loitering in the bank's foyer. He had been there awhile but had made no attempt to enter the bank. What piqued the tellers' attention was the fact that the man was wearing a ski mask. Officers arrived on the scene and questioned the man, who claimed he was wearing the mask because it was cold. It *was* cold outside, so that *could* explain the mask; but what the man couldn't explain was why he was carrying a BB pistol in his pocket and a note reading, "Give me all your money or I'll shoot you."

When a teller in Swansea, Massachusetts, told a would-be bank robber she had no money, he fainted. He was still unconscious when the police arrived. When the police found his getaway car, they discovered that the keys were locked inside it.

I'M MAD AS HELL AND I'M NOT GOING TO TAKE IT ANYMORE!

A woman in St. Louis was sitting in her car when the passenger door suddenly opened and a man jumped in holding a knife. The man bared his teeth and demanded that the woman hand over all her money, or else. "No way," said the woman as she shifted her weight to her right and punched the man square in the mouth. The impact from the unexpected blow knocked our villain back against the seat, and he accidentally cut himself with his own knife. The conked carjacker dropped the knife to the floorboard and clutched his wound. The woman quickly reached over, picked up the knife, and held it to the crook's throat until the police arrived. Was she an off-duty police officer, a young, strong female wrestler? Nope. She was a pissed-off seventy-seven-year-old grandmother who apparently didn't cotton to these young whippersnappers and their tomfoolery.

ONE SMALL STEP FOR MAN

*L*os Angeles County police were summoned by an emergency call to Ricks Liquor Store on a break-in complaint. Police arrived to find a twenty-three-year-old man alone in the locked store. "When they got there, they could see him sitting on the floor by the front counter, smoking a cigarette and drinking a beer," said Sergeant John O'Neal. "The cigarettes and the lighter were his." The burglar had helped himself to a beer from a case stacked on the floor. The police quickly surmised that the thief had cut a hole in the roof and entered the building through the air ducts. "After a few minutes, he realizes he can't get back out. So what do you think he does? He calls 911," Los Angeles police sergeant Roger Ferguson said. "The 911 operator at first didn't believe him. She thought it was a joke." But the sequestered suspect finally convinced the dispatcher, and she alerted the police. The store's owner was called to open the metal gate and door. He told police that two other burglars in the past two years had used the same method to get in–they couldn't get out either–but this criminal was the first to call the police.

A SLOW STING

A man in Bayreuth, in southern Germany, reached into his pocket and pulled out a mobile-telephone number that had been given to him by a police officer the previous year. The officer had told the man that the phone number was that of a much-sought-after drug dealer. Now the man wanted to buy some amphetamines and decided to call the high-powered contact. He punched in the number, ordered twenty-five grams of speed, and set up a meeting place for the deal. When he arrived at the location, two undercover officers promptly arrested him. Seeing how slowly the man's mind worked, maybe he needed the drugs just to get up to speed.

An Egyptian man carjacked a vehicle and drove it several miles before pulling over to the side of the road and leaving with the car's stereo system. The reason the man decided not to steal the car? He was blind.

ON THE CUTTING EDGE

A convicted criminal being escorted to jail in St. Petersburg, Florida, somehow managed to escape and go on the lam. During his escape, however, he suffered several deep cuts to his feet, but even with the loss of blood the criminal was able to vanish into thin air, and the authorities didn't have a clue as to his whereabouts. They got their break from the most unexpected of places—the local hospital. The authorities at the hospital got suspicious of their most recent patient—not because of his wounds but because of his words. When asked to fill out the standard hospital forms, on the line about the cause of the injury our escapee wrote, "Escape from jail."

*An attempted robbery of the Household Federal
Savings Bank in Reston, Virginia, ended
when a teller, after reading the robber's holdup
note, reached across the counter and punched
the man in the face, sending him racing
from the building.*

THE LETTER OF THE LAW

*T*he sheriff of Fincastle, Virginia, opened a letter addressed to him and was shocked and horrified at what he read. The letter, with no lack of detail, threatened to torture and kill the sheriff and the members of his family. It was obvious from the return address that the author of the letter was already a resident at the jail, so he was approached about the letter. The convict claimed he meant no harm with the letter but was simply doing research as to whether the sheriff opened his own mail or not. For writing these few sentences, the convict had a few more years added to his sentence.

REACH OUT AND PUT THE TOUCH ON SOMEONE

An eighteen-year-old Ann Arbor, Michigan, man stole a car containing a cellular phone and was happily driving around town when the phone rang. He must have thought to himself, "It's my car, so the phone call must be for me," because he answered it. He heard a woman's voice on the other end, and she sounded nice. She said she was a friend of the woman who actually owned the phone and that she was a very lonely lady and would love to meet a nice young man. The thief thought he'd hit the jackpot: a new car, a new cell phone, and a date with a lonely stranger. He set up a time to meet the mysterious woman and, being the gentleman he was, showed up on time, driving the stolen car and holding the stolen cell phone. The mystery of the mystery caller was soon solved when a police-woman approached the man and placed him under arrest. I wonder if, when he saw his date dressed as a police officer, he thought, "Is this real or is she just kinky?" Either way, the next cell phone he used was the phone in his cell.

WHO LET THE DOGS OUT?

*T*wo men in Newark, New Jersey, were arrested after they stole a shipping container with the word BEEFEATERS across the front. These two must have thought they'd lucked out–a huge crate filled with bottles of premium gin that they could quickly and easily sell on the black market. The only problem with their plan was the *s*. What do I mean? Well, the name of the gin is Beefeater–without an *s*. So what did the thieves wind up stealing instead? Seven hundred and ninety-nine cases of toy dog bones. The owner of the dog-bone company, Steven Mendal, stated that this was the second robbery within two months by illiterate criminals. If anyone out there knows the street value of toy dog bones, I'm sure these fellows would like to know.

ROOM SERVICE

Police in Portland, Oregon, received an emergency 911 call from a man staying at a local Howard Johnson Motel about mysterious intruders in his room. The thirty-three-year-old told the police that someone was trying to break into his second-floor room and hide under his bed. When the police arrived, the man jumped to the ground from the second floor and injured his back. The police searched his room but didn't find any intruders; what they did find was some heroin and cocaine. The man was taken to Brighton Medical Center for evaluation. I know the man was in possession of drugs, but it also sounded like he was possessed himself.

Police shot a man who was caught attempting to rob a grocery store after he charged them in an attempt to escape. According to the police, the man ran toward them with his index finger extended and yelled, "Bang! Bang!"

THE JOKE IS ON HIM

*C*ounterfeiting is a crime most people associate with criminals who have above-average intelligence and a certain level of skill. However, one Orlando, Florida, man's counterfeiting scheme went against that stereotype when he printed several million zlotys (Polish currency), for a total worth not more than $300. What put the man's black-market operation in the red was the fact that the machine he purchased to print the counterfeit zlotys cost $19,000. A Secret Service agent who was responsible for the arrest said, "He could have printed a boxcar full of them and not have enough to buy an expensive suit." The man won't have to worry about buying a suit for a while–because his clothes are now courtesy of the Florida prison system.

ARMED AND DANGEROUS

A bank robber carrying a crossbow, an ax, a stun gun, a smoke grenade, and a can of Mace walked into a bank in Osaka, Japan, and declared a holdup. He told the frightened tellers that he was prepared to use his entire arsenal if they didn't come across with the money. Fearing for their lives, the clerks gave the man $1,120,000; he grabbed it and made his escape. Unfortunately for the robber, but fortunately for the bank, the crook was so loaded down with weapons that he tripped and was quickly apprehended by a passerby. Too much of a good thing is a bad thing.

"I robbed from the rich, kind of like Robin Hood, except I kept it."

Career criminal Bill Becker summing up his life of crime.

THOSE ZANY, WACKY PRISONER LAWSUITS

- Jose Rivera Martinez, an inmate in Schenectady, New York, filed a $750,000 lawsuit against the county jail claiming he was allergic to the jail-issued hot dogs. His lawsuit alleged that the hot dogs he was forced to eat made him develop warts, which permanently disfigured him.

- Ernesto Mota filed a $7 million lawsuit claiming that the police in Oak Forest, Illinois, acted negligently after his arrest. Mota swallowed a bag of cocaine that was to be used as evidence against him, and subsequently suffered severe brain damage. He alleged that the police should have stopped him, or at least helped him receive medical attention more quickly.

- New York inmate David Degondea, who killed a police officer, filed a $3 million lawsuit seeking damages because he was injured during the arrest and could no longer work. Degondea's only source of income was selling drugs.

CAN'T WE JUST GET ALONG?

*J*ohn Esposito, who was being held in the Suffolk County
Correctional Center on Long Island for kidnapping, always
felt like a pawn when he played chess with the prisoner in the
next cell–alleged serial killer Joel Rifkin. Rifkin, who was linked
to at least nineteen murders, and Esposito would challenge each
other to chess matches through the bars of their adjoining cells,
but Esposito always lost. Andrew Siben, Esposito's lawyer,
checked the chess-playing escapades by telling his client, "It's
not good for your morale to get beaten by a serial killer." And
there's nothing worse than a kidnapper with low self-esteem.

In Columbia, Missouri, a man failed in his attempt to rob a grocery store using a socket wrench as his only weapon.

ACID REFLUX

*H*e was able to actualize himself up the tree but was not able to actualize himself down the tree" was the explanation given by High Point, North Carolina, police officer Gordon Snaden. The officer was referring to an incident involving a man who had ingested LSD and was found stranded naked in a tree.

PULL A HEIST AND PULL MY FINGER

A man and his wife were sleeping soundly in the bedroom of their Fire Island, New York, home when they heard noises in the house. They jumped out of bed to investigate, but although they thoroughly searched the house, they couldn't find the source of the noise. As they were preparing to go back to bed, they heard the unmistakable sound of flatulence coming from behind a closet door. They threw open the door and discovered a gaseous and bloated burglar hiding in the closet. They held the cramping career criminal, and their noses, until the police arrived. I don't know if they struck up a conversation, but I'll bet they struck a match.

A burglar in Union City, California, was startled when the homeowner returned, and dashed out of the house, over a fence, and into a neighbor's yard. The burglar, who, for some reason, was completely naked, was quickly captured after his leap over the fence landed him in the neighbor's cactus garden.

MAKING A BAD CALL

Some inmates, having so much time on their hands, find creative ways of whiling away the hours: they read or write books, file frivolous lawsuits, work out, make notes on their memoirs, learn a new occupation, and so on. But one curious inmate, serving time for a gas station robbery, was preoccupied with why he had never been prosecuted for a bank robbery for which he had previously been arrested and charged. The convict called the county attorney's office and asked about the oversight. The prosecutor did some research and discovered that the curious convict's file had been misplaced and that there were only a few months remaining before the statute of limitations ran out. The criminal, who was already serving ten years, plea-bargained with the DA to tack an additional ten years onto his sentence.

While attempting to rob a Long Island jewelry store at gunpoint, the 350-pound thief tripped and fell to the floor. He was still trying to get to his feet when the police arrived.

DRIVEN TO DISTRACTION

*P*olice in Lexington, North Carolina, arrived at the scene of a single-car accident and immediately arrested the three occupants. The men were charged with robbing a pedestrian and a gas station attendant just minutes before their accident. The accident was caused by the driver's attempt to make a speedy getaway while at the same time counting the stolen money.

GETTING SHORTCHANGED

*P*olice in Burlingame, California, were called out to investigate a burglary at the Towles Coffee Shop. The owners of the store kept things locked up after closing, and the burglar had had a hard time finding anything worth stealing. The police surmised that he'd made several attempts at breaking into a locked metal cabinet but was ultimately unsuccessful (the cabinet contained toilet paper anyway). Finally, not wanting to leave empty-handed and be the laughingstock of the burglary community, he stole the money from the "penny cup," which was located next to the cash register. The thief got away with about thirty cents in change. I hope he didn't spend it all in one place.

TWO WILL GET YOU TWENTY

*A*rmed robbery is a serious offense, regardless of the amount of money or merchandise stolen, as two young criminals in Florence, Oregon, found out. They targeted a man and approached him with their weapons drawn, demanding money. The man claimed he was broke, so the two thieves settled for stealing a couple of cigarettes from the man. They were arrested, charged with armed robbery, and now face as much as twenty years behind bars. Once inside the jail the two shouldn't have any trouble finding as many cigarettes as they want.

Police in Long Hill Township, New Jersey, are on the lookout for a serial doorbell thief.

LANDING IN THE ROUGH

Police helicopters were patrolling the skies looking for a man who had robbed a woman earlier in the day. The chase had been on for hours and the suspect had done a great job of eluding the police; his two accomplices, however, had already been captured. The Miami Shores, Florida, police captain said the man had the chance of being "the one guy that might have gotten away." Unfortunately, he was too polite. He was discovered by a stroke of luck—well, actually, a slice of luck. A golfer had sliced the ball off the tee and it had landed deep in the woods. As he was wandering around looking for his ball, he heard a voice from above: "Hey, hey, your ball is over there." The golfer looked up into a large tree and saw a man hiding among the branches. He quickly deduced from the helicopters searching the area that he should notify the police. He did, and when the police arrived, the man was more "up a tree" than he had been before. A lesson learned: keep your eye on the ball and your mouth shut.

GIVING SOMEONE THE BIRD

A woman and a parrot walk into a bar. It sounds like the beginning of a joke, doesn't it? Well, in a sense it is. Patrons of a Minneapolis, Minnesota, bar watched as a woman entered the bar with a box under her arm. The woman opened the box and showed everyone a beautiful parrot, which she then offered to sell. One of the patrons looked in the box and remarked on the splendor and beauty of the parrot. The man knew all about this particular breed of parrot, he told her, because he had one at home that looked exactly like it. The man finished his drink and went back to his house only to discover that—you guessed it—his parrot was missing. He informed the police, who went back to the bar and discovered the woman still there and still trying to hock the bird. The man got his bird back and the woman got put in the cage.

*An early-morning robbery of a Burger King
in Portland, Connecticut, ended abruptly when
the thief thought he heard an alarm go off
and left the store empty-handed. According to
the restaurant's manager, Jorge Ruisanchez,
the robber "disappeared in two seconds" after
hearing what turned out to be the timer
going off on the microwave oven.*

ZERO PERCENT INTEREST

*T*he customers and staff of a bank in Ishioka, Japan, were unimpressed when a seventeen-year-old boy and his sixteen-year-old girlfriend brandished a pair of kitchen knives and threatened a holdup. The boy walked up to a customer and held out the knife, but the man shook his head and walked away. Our rebuffed robber then turned his attention to the teller and flashed his knife menacingly. The boy's girlfriend was disgusted at the poor job he was doing and started telling him so in no uncertain terms. The two cutlery-carrying criminals then got into a lovers' brawl in front of the entire bank. Their argument grew to such an intensity that they didn't notice that one teller had triggered the bank's silent alarm. When the police arrived, they found the young man standing in the middle of the bank, still wielding his knife and begging someone to please give him some money. His girlfriend was by then telling him to hurry it up.

MAKING A HOUSE CALL

*I*n most cases a home robbery takes less than seven minutes, from the time the house is entered until the burglar leaves with your valuables. But in one case a burglar in Sandown, New Hampshire, realized he had some time on his hands and took advantage of it. The burglar literally made himself at home: he took a leisurely swim in the backyard pool, cooked himself a dinner of pork chops and Tater Tots, and loaded up the home-owner's truck with a BB gun and a watch. (Not a big haul—but who knows what stupidity lurks in the hearts of men?) Even with all the time spent on extracurricular activities, our "stay-at-home robber" nearly got away. The homeowner returned and caught the burglar trying in vain to get the truck started. He went from having a lot of time to serving a lot of time.

IT'S NOT AN INTELLIGENCE TEST

A man and woman arrested for the robbery of the Everett, Massachusetts, Co-op Bank were also suspects in at least eight other successful bank robberies. Getting a confession from the woman robber was easier than the police could have expected. According to Lieutenant Robert Botempo, "When I was booking this woman, I was asking her all the routine questions–you know: height, weight, age. For occupation, she said, 'Bank robber.'"

A twenty-four-year-old Texas man broke into a residence, stole a television set, and made a clean getaway. He was arrested a few hours later reentering the premises—he had forgotten to steal the television's remote control and came back to get it.

I'M NOT AS THINK AS YOU DRUNK I AM

A young man in York County, Pennsylvania, had been arrested earlier and sentenced to serve forty-eight hours in jail for driving while intoxicated. The man honored the judge's orders and showed up on time to serve out the full length of his sentence. He must have thought it was okay to have one for the road, though, because when he arrived at the jail, an officer thought he smelled alcohol on the man's breath and administered a blood-alcohol test. Sure enough, the man registered a .10–not as high as the reading that got him sentenced in the first place but enough to have his time in jail changed from forty-eight hours to thirty days. He should have remembered the old saying: Whiskey on beer, never fear; but beer before jail and you'll fail.

LIFE AIN'T SO BAD

*T*he hunt was on for an escaped murderer who had walked away from his minimum-security dormitory at the Chillicothe Correctional Institution in Ohio. The manhunt was in its second day when the police got a surprise tip. "We received a 911 phone call from [the escapee]. He said he was at a Shell station at I-71 and Route 35. He gave his name and birth date and said that he was the person we probably were looking for," Sheriff William R. Crooks said. Crooks and three deputies arrived at the service station and the exhausted escapee went quietly and without incident. "From the looks of him, he was tired, cold, and muddy," Crooks said. They sure don't make criminals the way they used to.

Two dim-witted thieves in Kazakhstan tried
to steal valuable copper wire from an electricity
cable in hopes of selling the metal on the
black market. Although the men didn't escape,
they will not be prosecuted for their offense—
because they tried to steal the wire while
the switch was on and ten kilovolts of electricity
was surging through the line.

I'M SO BLUE

A man from Miami, Florida, was stopped by a patrol car under suspicion of driving while intoxicated and given a field sobriety test. He failed the test, but he claimed he wasn't drunk, so the police took him to headquarters to perform a Breathalyzer test. The supposedly sauced suspect asked if he could use the rest room before he took the Breathalyzer (apparently tests made him nervous), and the police agreed. After a longer than normal time the police entered the rest room to see if the man was all right. He wasn't. He was lying on the floor, jerking around, with blue foam spewing from his mouth. Was he having a bizarre seizure? Nope. Apparently the man ate a blue urinal deodorant cake, assuming it would cover up any telltale signs of alcohol on his breath. The man was taken to the hospital, where a blood test revealed that he had a blood-alcohol level beyond the legal limit, and he was arrested for DUI. There was no way this criminal could talk his way out of a jail sentence—even though he was already blue in the face.

YOUR BRAIN—
DON'T LEAVE HOME WITHOUT IT

A pair of burglars successfully broke into an insurance office in Golden, Colorado, and proceeded to help themselves to the company's computer equipment. It was hard and sweaty work, and as they hadn't set off the alarm, they decided to take their time going about their chores. One of the criminals took off his jacket and threw it over a chair while he was disconnecting monitors from hard drives, unplugging power cords, and preparing to haul off nearly $30,000 in equipment. The other criminal, seeing how well things were going, decided to call his ex-wife in New Jersey on the company line. After their rest time the two loaded up the van and took off with a large load of valuable equipment. The first crook was arrested the following day–he'd remembered to take all the computer stuff, but he'd forgotten his jacket, which contained his pay stub in the front pocket. The second criminal was caught a few days later–had his accomplice ratted him out in order to get leniency? Nope. When the insurance company received their monthly phone bill, there was a charge to New Jersey at 2:45 in the morning. They traced the call to the second thief's ex-wife and she cooperated fully with the police. Calling your ex-wife while you're burglarizing a business–it seems like this fellow was just asking for it, doesn't it?

THREE STRIKES AND YOU'RE OUT!

*A*n old saying claims, "There is honor among thieves." Having waded into the shallow end of the criminal gene pool in collecting stories for this book, I doubt that this statement has any basis in reality. But I suppose it could be considered true in the case of one convenience-store robber in Fort Collins, Colorado. You see, our criminal had already robbed the same 7-Eleven store twice in one day, once in the morning and once in the afternoon. Apparently he wasn't very original, because he told the clerk, as he was leaving the store after the second robbery, that he would return later in the day to rob the store again. He wanted to give the clerk a break in between robberies so there would be more money in the cash register. Here's where the honor part comes in: true to his word, the same man entered the same 7-Eleven with the same intent–to rob the store. The only thing different was that there were several detectives in the store investigating the man's second robbery. Our virtuous villain was arrested on two counts of robbery and one count of attempted robbery.

YOU MAY ALREADY BE A WINNER . . .

*I*t's not one of the most common criminal teams, and this husband and wife duo were definitely not your typical Bonnie
and Clyde gangsters. But the manager and assistant manager of
a service station were surprised when a man and woman
entered the store, waved a gun in their faces, and threatened to
rob the place. The man took the manager at gunpoint into the
office, where the safe was located, while the woman stayed out
front holding the assistant manager at bay. Making small talk
during the robbery, the assistant manager told the woman about
the great contest the store was sponsoring and said that if she
completed an entry form, she might win a slew of valuable
prizes. And that's just what she did. The woman quickly filled in
the blanks, using her real name, address, and phone number,
crossed her fingers for good luck, and handed the form to the
assistant manager. The couple was sent on an all-expenses-paid
trip–up the river.

CROSSING A LINE

The police in Valley Springs, California, received a cellular-phone-call complaint from a motorist about a dangerous truck driver on the road. The motorist explained that the truck in front of him was crossing the centerline, driving erratically, swerving, and weaving back and forth. A patrol car spotted the truck in question and motioned for him to pull over. The trucker obliged and stopped his vehicle on the side of the road. The Good Samaritan who'd called in the complaint also pulled over and parked behind the truck. One police officer approached the truck slowly, making a note of the license plate and the driver number, then walked to the cab to talk with the driver. The trucker was very cooperative and showed absolutely no signs of being intoxicated or under the influence of narcotics. The police then decided to speak with the man who had called in the complaint, and that's when they found the real source of the problem. The driver of the car was intoxicated, very intoxicated; he registered at twice the legal limit. What the driver in his stupor didn't realize was that the truck was driving in a straight line–he was the one that was swerving all over the road. This is another reason why people shouldn't drink and dial.

GIVING THE KIDNAPPER THE FINGER

A shoe designer from Tokyo was so desperate for money, or attention, that he decided to pull off a kidnapping. And he knew the perfect victim–himself. The man made several phone calls to his family and mailed eight threatening letters, demanding fifty million yen for his return. To let them know he meant business, in the seventh letter, he sent his left ring finger and a final threat that the kidnapper (himself) would kill him if they didn't pay the money. The thirty-six-year-old self-napper was arrested after the police got word that a man had entered the emergency room with his left ring finger missing. The police traced the fingerprints left at the hospital; they matched those of the fake kidnapper. This isn't the first time that a stupid criminal has fingered himself.

A ROBBERY THAT WENT DOWN THE DRAIN

A clerk at a Baltimore, Maryland, convenience store looked up and found herself staring straight down the barrel of a loaded handgun. At the other end of the handgun a fidgety robber demanded all the money in the register. The cashier obliged and started handing over the cash. She noticed that the man was sweating slightly and rocking from foot to foot. She knew he was more than just nervous: he was displaying the nearly involuntary movements of someone who had to go to the bathroom–in layman's terms, the pee-pee dance. The incontinent convenience-store robber made it clear that before he went on the lam he had to go to the john. The clerk pointed him toward the bathroom, and the man quickly duckwalked down the aisle. While he was paying nature a visit, the clerk paid the police a call. The man was really pissed off when the police arrested him as he left the store, effectively slamming the lid shut on his criminal career.

In Italy, a man who was sentenced to six years in jail for aggravated robbery escaped incarceration by fleeing the country. After two years on the lam the man was arrested after he reentered his country. He was asked by the authorities why he'd risked arrest by returning to Italy; the man confessed that he had "missed the pizza."

HE WAS JUST A FIFTH WHEEL

A drug dealer in Jacob Lake, Arizona, found himself stranded
on the side of the highway after his car broke down. He
flagged down a passing truck driver, who was kind enough to
pull his rig off the road and offer the stranded motorist a ride.
The man said he didn't want to leave all of his personal items in
the car for fear they would be stolen and asked if he could take
some stuff with him in the truck's cab. The driver said he understood completely—you can't trust anyone these days. The
motorist was thankful, and in a few minutes he was back with
his arms filled with stuff: some clothes, a shaving kit, some of
this and some of that, and, of course, a spare tire. The man
insisted that he needed to bring along the spare tire and asked
the truck driver just to drop him off at a local motel. The driver
pulled into the motel parking lot and watched as the man
walked toward his room, rolling the spare tire in front of him.
Now, people have taken strange things inside their motel rooms
before, but a spare tire got the driver's attention and he thought
he would bring it to the attention of the police. The police,
upon inspecting the tire, found eleven pounds of marijuana hidden inside it. Now the drug dealer had better hope he's got
another kind of spare—spare time, that is, and lots of it.

A FAMILY GATHERING

Robert Palmer was arrested and charged with burglary in Savannah, Georgia, after removing a windowpane and entering the residence of Joseph Palmer. When the police detained him, he claimed he hadn't planned to rob the place; he was only curious as to whether he and Joseph Palmer were related. They're not.

A man held up a Toronto, Ontario, gas station wearing a pair of women's panties over his head to hide his identity. He was quickly apprehended because in order to make himself heard by the clerk, he stuck his face through one of the leg openings.

A DAY LATE AND A DOLLAR SHORT

A twenty-four-year-old Detroit Lakes, Minnesota, man was arrested and charged with the attempted robbery of a convenience store. According to prosecutors, the robber wanna-be stopped a customer on his way into the store and handed him a dollar. The criminal told the man he intended to rob the store but didn't have a proper disguise and asked if the fellow would be so kind as to buy him a handkerchief that he could use to hide his face. The man took the dollar, walked into the store, and told the clerk about the odd encounter outside, and the clerk notified the police. No mention about what happened to the dollar.

AN OPEN-AND-SHUT CASE

A young would-be car thief broke into a garage in Waskom, Texas, and snuck into the owner's van with the intention of stealing it. Apparently the thief wasn't mechanically inclined, because as he was fumbling around trying to hot-wire the car, he accidentally activated the electric locks–and couldn't find the right button to open them. He was making so much noise frantically pushing every button he could find to open the door that he woke the owners. When the police arrived, they found the suspect still locked in the van. And with this type of criminal mentality a prison escape is entirely unlikely.

A market in Greensboro, North Carolina, was robbed by two men—one of them brandishing a pitchfork.

MORE ZANY, WACKY PRISONER LAWSUITS

- Moberly, Missouri, inmates Jimmie Perko and Neil Sleeper, upon being rearrested after they broke out of their medium-security prison, filed a lawsuit against the state for $1.8 million. They claimed they'd escaped because prison was too dangerous and the state had done nothing to protect them. "A person can only put up with this constant fear for so long until he is forced to seek safety," alleged their lawsuit.

- Michigan inmate Randy Parson won a settlement of $1.7 million in a "failed to prevent suicide attempt" lawsuit. Parson botched his suicide attempt and is still serving fifteen to thirty for murder.

- Randy Kraft, a convicted serial killer, filed a $60 million defamation lawsuit against Warner Books and the author of the book *Angel of Darkness*. Kraft, a death-row inmate convicted of the sexual torture and murder of sixteen men, claimed the book cast him in an unfair light by portraying him as a "sick, twisted" man.

THE CHECK'S IN THE JAIL

A man in Auburn, California, was arrested and charged with burglary, forgery, and passing bad checks after purchasing $267 worth of supplies from an office store. The man had painstakingly printed bogus checks, complete with false bank account numbers that could successfully be scanned through any store's "check identification" system. So where did our crafty counterfeiter go wrong? For some unknown reason, the man had printed his full and proper name and address on every check. Pay to the order of: Idiot.

One career criminal was killed when he and another man got into a fight over who had the longest criminal record.

RUN FOR COVER

*A*n Angolan man had the patrons and staff of a Madrid, Spain, café trembling as he shouldered his weapon and looked down the barrel. It was a daring midday robbery, and the armed man had the drop on everyone, demanding their money lest he open fire on them. It was then that an observant waiter recognized the make and model of the weapon the robber had— it was a 1998 black umbrella. "At first, people thought it was a rifle and then a waiter noticed it was a fake," a police spokesperson said. Waiters rushed the dumb-fella with the umbrella and quickly disarmed him.

A man stole a vehicle from the Hastings, Nebraska, city storage shed and drove it to a local convenience store to buy a case of beer. Upon arriving at the store the man paid for the beer and filled up the vehicle with gas before returning home. The clerk, suspecting that the man was drunk, alerted the police and described both the man and the vehicle. A few days before, the city had experienced a major snowstorm, and our drunk driver had stolen the only thing he knew would get him to the store—a snowplow.

THE STUPID CROOK BOOK

THE REAL MR. MONEYBAGS

*R*obbing an armored truck is a very dangerous heist; the guards are heavily armed, and the truck is virtually impenetrable. But an armored truck in Memphis, Tennessee, was successfully robbed as the truck guard was about to enter a supermarket to make a pickup. Two gunmen approached him, put their guns in the driver's face, took the large canvas bag he was carrying, and made their getaway. The bag was fairly light, but it was definitely filled with something. The crooks stopped a short distance away to check out their booty and were sadly disappointed. Remember, the guard was making a pickup, so the only thing stuffed in the large canvas moneybag . . . was a stack of other large canvas moneybags.

THE FAT OF THE LAND

*T*he getaway is one of the most important parts of any successful bank robbery. One needs to have the proper vehicle
ready and running, make sure there's gas in the tank, have a
fairly well planned escape route, and so on. But one robber
thought he would just wing his escape–or, actually, foot it. A
man in Fremont, California, had accomplished the first part of a
bank robbery–the initial "Give me all the money" bit. He took
the money and headed out the door intending to run "wee, wee,
wee" all the way home. Passersby, who saw the man exit the
bank with the money, however, had a different idea and gave
chase. After less than a block the robber gave up his sprint to
freedom and slowed down to a leisurely walk. Was he confident
that he had gotten away? Nope. You see, the suspect was only
five foot six and weighed well over three hundred pounds. Our
rotund robber needed a rest, and the sentencing judge was more
than glad to give him several years to catch his breath.

A shoplifter at the Tom Tom CDs & Tapes Store in St. George, Utah, was seen stuffing a CD under his shirt and was stopped by the clerk. The thief tore free, bolted through the door, and ran face-first into a pillar in front of the store, knocking himself unconscious.

DON'T BE A LITTERBUG

Cops in a patrol car in Los Angeles observed a vehicle swerving on and off the road, crossing the centerline, and driving very erratically over all. They popped on the lights and began pursuit. When the driver of the car realized the police were hot on his tail, he tried to throw a beer can out the window—an obvious sign that the man was very intoxicated. He was so intoxicated, in fact, that he had a hard time getting the can through the window. He thought the logical thing to do would be to make the opening bigger—so he opened his car door in order to throw the can out. He was successful in tossing the can out of the speeding car; he just forgot to let go of it. The man bounced down the road but was left with only minor scrapes and bruises . . . no word on the condition of the beer can.

A man who was suffering from amnesia asked the police in Hamburg, Germany, to help him find out his identity. He wished he hadn't done that when the police discovered that he was wanted for fraud and arrested him.

NOTHING RUNS LIKE A DEER

*N*ot unlike the previous story, this is a police chase that will go down in the annals of stupid-criminal history. A man from Gastonia, North Carolina, stole a vehicle and made his getaway. He knew the cops would pursue him, so he wanted to make sure he had a full tank of gas. His first stop was a local gas station, where he filled up the tank and then committed his second crime by not paying for the gas. The driver put the pedal to the metal and hit the road, pushing the limits of the engine in order to put distance between him and the coppers. There was a gap of thirty minutes between the first crime of stealing the vehicle and the second crime of stealing the gas before the police were alerted to the criminal's activities by a call from the gas station attendant. They jumped in their patrol cars, strapped on their seat belts, hit the blue lights, and sped out of the parking lot. They soon spotted the man, as he had pulled the stolen vehicle off the road and was now driving down the sidewalk. The police cut in front of the man and forced him to stop and kill the ignition. Why did the chase last such a short time? Well, the vehicle the man had stolen was a bright red Troy-Bilt riding lawn mower. The man was arrested and charged with stealing the lawn mower and the gas and resisting arrest. Of course, he might make a deal with the judge to trim his sentence.

HITTING THE WRONG NOTE

*K*evin McCarthy, a clerk at a Check Exchange, taught one would-be robber that a copy of Strunk and White's *The Elements of Style* is a crucial resource manual when preparing a proper holdup note. The clerk became suspicious of the man when he first saw him pacing outside the exchange. "Before he came in, I thought he was a funny-looking guy, with a dark wig, a funny glue-on mustache, glue-on sideburns, a long dark coat, a baseball cap, and a duffel bag. He handed me a Western Union slip that was just a bunch of gibberish. I didn't even try to read it—it was just ridiculous," McCarthy said. "I was just about to tell him, 'You'll have to rewrite this,' when he pulled out a shoe box with some red sticks that looked like dynamite inside." The irate illiterate thrust the note back at the clerk, who was seated comfortably behind inch-thick bulletproof glass, and asked, "Can you read that?" "I said no and hit the alarm button," recalled McCarthy. The man stormed out of the exchange swearing loudly—he was not apprehended. No one is sure whether the shoe box contained dynamite or flares, but one thing is certain: the man definitely had a short fuse.

CHOKING ON HIS OWN WORDS

A man convicted of kidnapping and robbery tried to get his sentence overturned by claiming that the witnesses' identification of him shouldn't have been entered at the trial. When the New Haven, Connecticut, police officers arrested the man, he declared himself innocent of all charges and asked to be released. However, he resisted going back for a "one-on-one face-off," a procedure in which the suspected criminal is brought to the scene of the crime for identification purposes. The man claimed it was a waste of time to take him back, because he was innocent; furthermore, he stated, "How can they identify me? I had a mask on."

A man robbed a post office in Cariato, Italy, and made off with L3,000. He ran outside and discovered that his getaway car, which he had left running, had been stolen.

A SIX-PACK SHY OF A CASE

*A*n inebriated man in Longmont, Colorado, had just finished off his third six-pack but still had a thirst for more brew. So he jumped into his car and drove to the same convenience store where he had bought his original three sixers–I suppose he wanted to make it an even case. When he got there, he had the idea of getting the beer at a discount: a five-fingered discount. So he got out a crowbar and started working drunkenly on the front door, trying to pry it open, but even through his hazy, bloodshot eyes, he could tell something was wrong–the store was still open. Customers inside the store stared in amazement at the man working feverishly to open the door and, thinking he might need some help, they called the police. Once the man realized his mistake, he tried to make his escape, but search as he might he couldn't find the keys to his car. The police arrived and allowed the man to sober up in jail. It turned out that the reason he couldn't find his keys was that he had left them in the ignition.

A PATTY SHY OF A WHOPPER

It was shortly before eight in the morning when a man entered a Burger King in Ypsilanti, Michigan, and pulled out a gun. He demanded all the cash in the fast-food store and demanded it fast (and I'm not talking thirty minutes or less). The clerk explained that the drawers wouldn't open without a food order. So the robber asked for a burger and a side of onion rings. "Sorry," the clerk said, pointing to the clock, "those items are only sold after ten-thirty." Either not in the mood for breakfast or tired of not having things his way, the man pocketed the gun and slumped out of the store. Hold the pickles, hold the lettuce, special orders do upset us.

A robbery duo in Michigan entered a record shop and spastically waved their pistols. The first robber shouted, "Nobody move!" He noticed movement out of the corner of his eye and fired— shooting his fidgety partner.

HE WAS STUPID—TO COIN A PHRASE

A man broke into a rare-coin shop and looked in amazement at the different sizes and shapes of coins set out in display cabinets throughout the store. He needed to know which coins were worth the most, as it would help him set a price when he resold them. He spotted a book detailing the various grades and values of rare coins and picked it up, had a seat, and started thumbing through the volume. I suppose a book about old coins must be pretty boring, because soon the man fell fast asleep. That's how the police found him the next morning . . . sleeping soundly with the book of coin values lying open on his lap. The man, like some of the coins he had been reading about, was taken out of circulation.

HANDBAGGED

A woman in Stratford, Ontario, was in a supermarket doing a little shopping for women's wallets–other women's wallets. The woman looked innocent enough, strolling around the supermarket with a shopping cart, but her eyes weren't on produce but on purses. She would wait until an unsuspecting shopper was looking the other way and then quickly relieve her of her wallet. She soon felt she was under surveillance and decided to take the stolen wallets out of her purse, throw all four of them into a waste bin, and leave the store. At home, the woman breathed a sigh of relief as she settled onto her couch to watch a little television. She got up to answer a knock at the door and was surprised to find the police there to arrest her for robbery. How had they tracked her down? It turns out the woman had stolen only three wallets that day–the fourth wallet she'd thrown away was her own.

*A young woman in Lake City, Florida, was
arrested for attempting to hold up a Howard
Johnson Motel with a chain saw. Fortunately
for the clerk, the chain saw was electric . . .
and wasn't plugged in.*

HI-HO, QUICKSILVER, AWAY!!!

*T*wo young men in Texarkana, Arkansas, became big hits with their friends when they showed up with a shiny, silver-white liquid that looked really cool. The boys played with the magic liquid, watching in amazement as it beaded up on their arms when they dipped them into the container, then poured it on the floor and stared as it shimmered and danced. When asked where they got such great stuff, the boys answered that they'd stolen it from an abandoned neon-sign plant. They had several containers of the liquid, and they said they would gladly share it with their friends. What the boys didn't realize was that the liquid was highly poisonous mercury—used in the production of neon signs. The two were arrested for breaking and entering, and their little idiotic experiments forced the evacuation of ten homes, the temporary closing of their high school, the medical treatment of more than sixty people, and the shutting down of a Subway sandwich shop. It's interesting that the boys stole mercury, which is, of course, named after the Greek god Mercury . . . who is the god of travel, commerce, and thievery.

THE THREE STOOGES

*I*t was a plan intended to make them all millionaires—a great con, they thought; a clever scam, they giggled; a dumb idea, actually. Three inmates at New York's Rikers Island Prison worked in tandem to hatch a plot to smuggle a gun inside the prison walls. One of the inmates had a day job and was able to successfully bring the loaded weapon onto the prison grounds and into his cell. Were they planning on breaking out? Nope. Here's the plot: One of the inmates would take the gun the other inmate brought in and shoot the third inmate in the leg. The wounded inmate would then sue the prison for "negligence" in allowing a gun to be smuggled into the prison in the first place. They would then, as part of their settlement agreement, all be released from prison and collect "millions" in damages. Did it work? Part of it did—the part where one inmate shoots another in the leg. But the lawsuit never made it to trial, all three men are still behind bars, and one of them is now called Gimpy.

LOWERING THE BAR

A man who was recently released on bail for an armed robbery was looking for some fast cash to support his drug
habit. He lived in a small apartment just above a tavern and
thought that of all the places to hold up, the bar would require
the least amount of effort. The man entered the darkly lighted
Philadelphia bar with his gun drawn, went to the bartender, and
demanded the day's take from the register. The bartender
quickly obliged, handing him all the cash. The man took the
money and ran back upstairs to his apartment. Ten minutes
later, a knock on the door revealed to the man, who was sitting
at the kitchen table counting his money, that he had already
been tracked down. His main problem? Not only did he live
upstairs from the bar, but also the bartender was his landlord,
who, of course, had no trouble identifying the man and giving
the police his current address.

DUMB ON ALL ACCOUNTS

We are all concerned about terrorists, bomb scares, and threats to our airlines–but if all terrorists were as stupid as this guy, we wouldn't have a care in the world. A South Carolina man claimed he had planted bombs at the airport terminals in both Columbia and Charleston and demanded $2 million to disclose their location, or else he would detonate them. He had obviously seen movies where undercover police officers stake out the area where the money drop-off occurs, so our "mad bomber" thought he would outsmart the police by changing the scenario. He told the authorities to deposit the $2 million in cash in his bank account, giving them the name of his bank and his account number. The police had no problem tracking down the address of the man who owned the bank account, and they made an arrest within minutes. The police did make a deposit, however; they deposited the man in the local jail.

FIRST COME, FIRST SERVED

It was a "meet the police" night in a Spokane, Washington, community and people were getting to know their local police officers while examining some of the latest in crime-fighting and law-enforcement technology. One new product on display was a driver's license computer connected directly to the state's main computer. The new technology, the demonstrating officer promised, could run a check using your driver's license and automatically bring up any outstanding tickets. To prove that it worked, he asked for volunteers. One guy came forward, whipped out his driver's license, smiled to the crowd, and waited as the officer ran his number through the new system. Well, the computer worked, all right. It showed that the vacuum-headed volunteer was a wanted criminal with several outstanding warrants for his arrest. The phrase "meet the police" had a different meaning to the man, as they arrested him on the spot.

A judge looked at his docket and called the next case: *PEOPLE VS. STEVEN LEWON CROOK.* When the judge was ready to see the defendant, he called, "Crook, come forward." Five prisoners left the holding cell and entered the courtroom.

ID ARE THE FIRST TWO LETTERS IN IDIOT

It was near midnight in Amherst, Massachusetts, when the police spotted a young man who appeared to be intoxicated sitting on a concrete wall. They approached the young man and asked for identification. It quickly became apparent that the young man's name was I. M. Screwed because instead of pulling out an ID, he accidentally pulled out a bag of marijuana.

A Nevada man who was wanted on outstanding warrants for fraud decided to make a new life for himself when he reached West Haven, Connecticut. As his first step in walking the straight and narrow, he applied for a job and was summarily arrested. Why? The position he applied for was with the local police department, which uncovered his record during a routine background check.

POT LUCK

A man entered his Boise, Idaho, home and immediately realized he had been robbed. He checked the house thoroughly, made up a list of the stolen merchandise, and called the police to report the crime. Once the officers were at the scene, they went over the list of stolen items: a VCR, a bong, and a marijuana pipe. The police stared at the man in disbelief but continued to fill out the robbery report. The man was slightly upset that his house had been burglarized, but he gloated about how stupid the robbers were, as they had overlooked a film canister filled with marijuana. The police asked the man to verify that the marijuana hadn't been stolen, and when he opened up the canister to show them the contents, they placed him under arrest for possession. The song says, "Smoke gets in your eyes," but this guy must have had enough smoke to cloud his ability to think.

UNDER WHERE?

The police in Klamath Falls, Oregon, received a call from a homeowner who had just been the victim of a robbery. Two officers responded immediately and took the statement of the homeowner. The victim said a man had broken into his house, knocked him to the floor, stolen several items from his home, and then left–and oh, by the way, the thief was only wearing his underwear. Apparently the robber had removed his pants and shirt in the homeowner's front yard before entering the house, under the assumption that it would be harder to identify him. In his haste to escape, the underwear-wearing robber had forgotten to take the shirt and pants he had left in the front yard. When the police examined the pants, they found, in the back pocket, the man's wallet and photo ID. So the man's robbery attire and his career as a thief were the same: brief.

A man robbed a liquor store in the Roswell area of New Mexico. Although he wore a bag over his head, the police got an excellent description of the perpetrator—he was wearing a plastic bag.

A SURPRISE ATTACK

*I*t was nice outside and we decided to open up the front door," Jeff Broxon said. Jeff and his wife, Melane, put up a baby fence in their front door so their two dogs couldn't get out but they could still enjoy the weather. "I was sitting in a recliner drinking iced tea and my wife had just sat down on the couch with a bowl of ice cream." That's when it happened. Suddenly, a robber in a paper-bag mask leaped through the open front door of the Bradenton, Florida, home intending to surprise the couple inside and rob them. But the surprise was on him. "This guy comes jumping over this gate with a bag over his head," Jeff Broxon recalled. "He had a paper bag over his head with holes cut in it so he could see. He had a shirt over his arm like he was covering a gun, and he said, 'I'm going to blow your heads off if you don't give me your money.' I said, 'Okay, no problem.'"

Broxon carefully moved to one side and took out his wallet; he slowly opened it to reveal the contents to the would-be robber.

"I opened [the wallet] to draw attention away from my wife," he said.

Skeeter, one of the Broxons' dogs, provided further distraction by "running all over the place" and snapping at the robber's leg.

The intruder was so busy fighting off the dog and ogling the money in Broxon's wallet that he didn't notice that Melane had pulled out a .22-caliber pistol and had it pointed at his head.

Jeff smiled, the crook looked confused, Skeeter barked, and Melane kept the robber in her sights. "I looked at him and I said, 'Bud, I think you've had a bad day,'" Jeff said. "My wife had a gun pointed right at him," he continued. "She said, 'Freeze or you're dead.'"

Melane instructed the bandit to take off his mask and sit down on the floor with his hands on his knees. Jeff took the gun and Melane called 911. A few minutes later six carloads of police officers squealed in and arrested the unwanted guest.

"It was an interesting little evening," Jeff Broxon said. "The bad part of it was, we missed the end of the program we were watching." I've seen television lately, and I can't think of any show that would have been more interesting or more entertaining than that.

CALLING ALL CARS

*A*s the speeding car raced away from the scene of a Portland, Oregon, bank robbery, one alert citizen wrote down the number of the car's license plate. The police traced the number to what turned out to be the previous owner of the car–a man who, in fact, had sold the car to someone else earlier that year. The previous owner called the current owner and told him the police were asking questions about the whereabouts of the vehicle. In an unexplainable act of stupidity, the man who owned the car (a.k.a. "the Bank Robber") called the police to see what the problem might be. He told them that he was the current owner of the car and even gave them his correct street address–after which he was arrested for two bank robberies in the Portland area. The man was caught after the police put a make on his license plate, and now it'll be his responsibility to make license plates.

A man applying for a position at a Baltimore police station was handed the standard application form to fill out. On most job questionnaires there is a line about whether you've ever committed a crime. The man checked the "yes" box, and when asked by the officer in charge about his crime, the man admitted to carjacking a woman and robbing five people in Texas. Needless to say, he was arrested.

WARNING: NOT INTENDED AS A CHILD'S TOY

*E*mployees of the First Bank and Trust Co., in Princeton, Kentucky, were going about their business when a man approached one of the tellers, waved a pistol, and demanded all the money in the till. The teller looked at the robber's face and knew he was serious; then she looked at the weapon he was pointing and realized that he was seriously stupid, too. The man was brandishing a plastic toy gun. The teller refused to give the man anything except the cold shoulder. While he was arguing with this teller, another employee of the bank, who happened to have a Polaroid camera handy, took a picture of the robber. After he was caught on candid camera, the man backed away from the counter and said he was just kidding–he was actually there to get change for a hundred-dollar bill. When the police were taking the man away, they noticed a rolled-up stocking underneath his baseball cap; he had forgotten to pull it down over his face before the robbery. Even though the weapon was plastic, the man was still charged with armed robbery.

SHUTTING OUT THE BAD ELEMENTS

It was shortly after closing time at an Office Depot in Lennox, California, when a man who had been hiding in the store for an unknown amount of time came out of nowhere and declared he was going to rob the store. He hustled all the employees into an office and felt a sense of pride, knowing that everything was going according to plan, as he locked them securely away. He then quickly reviewed the steps of the plan: 1) Hide in the store–did that! 2) Get all the employees locked in an office–did that! 3) Open door, let partner in–that's next! 4) Clean out the place, ha, ha, ha. (Author's note: I made up that laugh part.) Seeing that he was at stage three, he trotted over to the back door, walked outside, and gave his buddy the all-clear sign. Of course, what he didn't notice was the ALL DOORS LOCK AUTO-MATICALLY sign on the inside of the door. Try as he might, he couldn't get back into the store. It's a clear-cut example of an open-and-shut case of stupidity.

Run for the Border: A bicycle bandit pedaled his bike to the drive-through window at a Fort Worth, Texas, Taco Bell and placed his order. He wanted all the money in the store . . . and a chalupa.

COOKING HIS OWN GOOSE

"Give me some money or I'll kill the goose," yelled an enraged thirty-three-year-old man in a Toronto, Ontario, doughnut shop. Frightened patrons turned to see the robber holding a goose under one arm, his other hand wrapped tightly around the goose's neck. Noticing the madness in the man's eyes, a kindly woman handed the would-be neck wringer six dollars. The man dropped the goose and ran. Two months later the animal assaulter was at it again. This time he was armed with a rock and a two-month-old baby raccoon. The man stopped people on the street and told them that if they didn't give him some money, he was going to bash in the raccoon kit's head. He said he would trade the life of the raccoon for about thirty-five dollars in cash. A passing pedestrian jumped on a local bus and told the driver to call the police. When the police arrived, the baby raccoon escaped from the kit-napper's arms and hid under their patrol car. At his first court appearance, the suspect tried to make a fashion statement by appearing before the magistrate without any clothes on. "Apparently he left here with his clothes, but he refused to put them on," said a police officer. As he was standing naked with a group of other criminals, I'm surprised the robber didn't get a goose of another kind.

NOTHING TO HIDE

A home owner saw two heavily armed men enter his house, so he immediately called 911 and fled his residence–smart move. The police arrived and began searching the man's house. They didn't find any suspicious men, but they did find something else suspicious: hospital clothes, surgical gloves, and masks. The police questioned the home owner on why armed men would have targeted his home for a robbery in the first place. The man claimed he didn't know and that he didn't have anything to hide; he even helped the police conduct the search. When they entered the bedroom, the helpful home owner lifted his bed slightly so the officers could get a quick peek underneath, and the mattress slid off. Sitting on top of the box spring wasn't a collection of girlie magazines but a huge pile of cash. The man had stretched a sheet of plastic over the box spring, laid his money on top of it, and covered the cash with another sheet of plastic. "It slid off, and the police looked at him and he said, 'So what, I sell drugs now and then,'" Deputy Police Chief Bill Guess rcalled. "Here we have the Guinness book of world records' dumbest criminal. He did everything for us, but if we hadn't been so thorough, it may have been just another home invasion." Evidence obtained from the search linked the man to six bank robberies. Since the gracious host was used to sleeping on a lumpy mattress, the one in prison will seem like home.

SPEED LIMIT

A trooper in Mayes County, Oklahoma, made a routine speeding stop, pulled out his ticket book, and approached the car. Now, police officers have heard every excuse for speeding you can imagine, but they'll always become suspicious if you constantly change your story–which is what this woman driver did. The officer, realizing that something was not right, asked for permission to search the woman's car. According to the trooper, the woman sputtered, "When . . . I mean . . . if you find dope in my car, what's going to happen?" Having probable cause to do a search, the trooper no longer needed the woman's permission, and he turned up a variety of drugs, including fifty grams of methamphetamine. Huh, fifty grams of methamphetamine–no wonder the woman was speeding.

A man attempted to rob a store in Natrona Heights, Pennsylvania, by threatening the clerk with a can of ravioli.

A YEN FOR MONEY

A man who was concerned about violating the terms of his driver's license, suspension from an earlier DUI case, decided not to drive his car to his next job. His next job, however, was the attempted robbery of the Shanghai Express Restaurant in Tampa, Florida. The conscientious criminal walked up to the drive-through window and demanded all the money in the restaurant–to go. When a car pulled up behind him at the window, the frightened fleet-footed felon fled. He was cornered a few blocks away by the police and given "free delivery" to the local jail.

Three men ran out into the street after robbing a Santa Ana, California, store and, like the horse thieves in the Westerns, fired their weapons in the air in celebration. When the men saw an approaching patrol car, one robber quickly thrust his gun into his trousers . . . but the gun went off and shot him in the genitals. He was easily apprehended—they weren't.

I'M NOT WHO I THINK I AM

*T*he police in Springfield, Illinois, pulled a young man over and cited him for driving without a license. When the officer asked him his name, the young man answered, "Johnny Rice." The officer was a little suspicious and asked the man to spell it for him–but the driver couldn't spell "Johnny" in any of the conventional ways. He then changed his mind and told the officer his real name. The police followed up on the suspicious fellow and contacted the car's owner. The owner of the car said that he had in fact loaned his friend the car and wasn't sure why he'd given the police a false name. A search was run on the man (using his real name, of course), and it turned out there were no warrants for his arrest and he wasn't wanted by the police on any matter–in fact, he had a clean record. Why he'd decided to give the officers a false name is something only, uh, only what's-his-name can answer.

BREAD CRUMBS ARE FOR THE BIRDS

Danny Foster's Bar, a drinking establishment in Hinton, West Virginia, was broken into one night, and the burglar took off with money, liquor, candy, and cigarettes (enough stuff to make a pretty nice weekend, if you ask me). The burglar apparently brought a pillowcase from home to stuff with the stolen swag; what he didn't realize was that one of the liquor bottles he'd swiped had shattered and cut a small hole in the pillowcase. The police on the scene simply followed the trail of liquor and coins to the burglar's house–just down the street. The hardest part of following a trail of coins was when the police came to a street corner–they had to turn on a dime.

A man who was pulled over and cited for not carrying a driver's license submitted to a routine search and was found to be carrying cocaine in his underwear. In order to absolve himself of any wrongdoing, the man claimed that the underwear he was wearing didn't belong to him.

GETTING A JUMP START ON A ROBBERY

Glenn Doolin, a tobacco farmer, pulled into his driveway, got out of his truck, and noticed two unfamiliar faces coming out of his house carrying some very familiar things—his stereo, compound bow, BB gun, and a pillowcase filled with jewelry. "I hollered at them, but they just kept on," Doolin said. "They never answered and then they got into their car. . . . When their car wouldn't start, they asked me if I wanted my stuff back, and they started unloading the stuff." Doolin was amazed and angered at seeing his possessions in the hands of someone else. "They started begging me not to call the police," Doolin said, but he did anyway. "Then they'd go back out and try to start the car, and the car wouldn't start, so they'd come back in and start begging. They must have done this four or five times," Doolin said. The stranded suspects finally asked Doolin if he would give their getaway car a jump start. Knowing their car was stalled, Doolin stalled the two thieves by saying he didn't have jumper cables but he'd run next door to borrow some. Then the hard-working farmer looked at the two men who were trying to take his possessions and decided to give them a piece of his mind. "I said, 'What's the matter with you?' I said, 'Look what you've done to the place.'" Doolin's pointed remarks got him something he didn't expect to see . . . his own loaded revolver pointed at his face. "I thought he was going to shoot me, but he just took the bullets from the gun and threw them out in the yard, and he said, 'Now we've done everything we can. . . . We'll even clean the place up.'" They began tidying up Doolin's house, begging him not to file a police report when the police arrived. Before they were hauled off, Doolin's curiosity got the best of him. He asked the robbers why they didn't run into the woods or take his truck, which still had the keys in the ignition, and even why they didn't shoot him to make their getaway. The two turned to look at the older man and said they weren't out to make a profit on the robbery. "They said they were just trying to steal enough to fix their car," recalled Doolin.

HE'S NOT SHARP ENOUGH TO CUT WARM BUTTER

A clerk working behind a lottery counter in Rochester Hills, Michigan, was threatened by a robber wielding a knife. Since the counter was between the two men, the clerk simply took a step back to be out of the way of the sharp knife and called security. The robber gave up, dropped the knife, and ran out of the store. Within minutes both the neighborhood and the store were swarming with police officers searching for the armed-robbery suspect. As the old saying goes, a criminal always returns to the scene of the crime, and it was true in this case, too. The man reentered the store a half hour later and asked if he could please have his knife back. He was tackled by security officers and arrested for attempted robbery. Why did the man risk arrest for a knife? Was it special? An antique? Nope. According to police sergeant Dennis Nash, "It was just a little paring knife." A paring knife isn't always the sharpest knife in the drawer–and neither was this guy.

WEIGHT AND SEE

On Christmas Day a few years ago, a man called 911 and stopped a burglary in progress . . . he was an eyewitness to what was happening, because he was the burglar. Apparently the man walked into a health center and hid in a bathroom until the business closed for the night. Much to his chagrin, he soon realized that the valuable equipment and medicines were locked up–so he started jamming office supplies into his pockets. Then a thought occurred to him: "If they locked the doors, how am I going to get out?" He couldn't. So he picked up the phone and called 911, telling them he had been "buzzed" into the building to use the bathroom and the guard had forgotten he was there and closed up for the night. There was only one problem: the building had no buzzer security system. The building did, however, have an alarm system, which the burglar had accidentally set off twice. Each time he'd answered the phone call from the security guard and told him everything was okay. Police officer Deborah Reinarman said the man confessed to her that he regretted calling 911 for help. "He said he should have just broken a window," she reported. Too bad the bewildered burglar hadn't called her earlier for advice.

WRONG PLACE, WRONG TIME, WRONG CRIME

I'm not making this up," said police spokesman Wayne Shelor of the Clearwater Police Department. What he was referring to was a misguided young Chicago man who chose the worst parking lot in the world to sell crack cocaine: the parking lot of the Clearwater Police Department. But this dealer must have been dealt a bad hand–and he was a few cards short of a deck. Not only did he pick the wrong parking lot, but he also tried to sell the crack to a police officer–in full uniform. He asked, "Do you want to buy some crack cocaine?" and then reached into his pocket and pulled out three rocks of crack.

So what had possessed a man to try to sell crack cocaine to a uniformed police officer, who was standing in the police station parking lot, surrounded by marked police cars, within sight of the police station? Shelor remembered the dealer's words: "He said, 'I knew I was taking a chance.'" Well, I guess the guy's going to get used to seeing uniformed police officers, surrounded by marked police cars, and so on . . . for a long time to come.

A grocery-store robbery in Calgary, Alberta, was hindered because of two things: 1) the robber's only weapon was an ordinary manual can opener; and 2) during the attempted getaway, the sixteen-month-old baby of the robber's girlfriend kept falling out of the stroller.

TAKE-OUT SERVICE

A St. Louis man who'd had a little too much to drink thought he would get something to eat and pulled his car up to what he thought was a drive-through restaurant. He drove up to the intercom and yelled his order. He soon realized that he'd ordered up a large portion of trouble–the man was yelling into the intercom of the Area III St. Louis police station. An officer came out, not wanting to see if the man wanted fries, but to see how fried he was–and arrested the driver for DUI. It's a good thing the man didn't ask to supersize it!

The follow-up on this story is that the next day a local radio DJ, "Wacky Pat" Fortune, wanting to play a prank for his listening audience, pulled up to the same intercom stand. A quick computer trace found that Fortune had several unpaid traffic tickets, and he was promptly arrested. ("Wacky"—yes; "Fortune"—no.)

THE FIRST SIGN OF STUPIDITY

A young entrepreneur in Baltimore, Maryland, looking to generate more sales, put up a sign announcing his wares on the side of a newspaper box. Two plainclothes police officers saw the unlawful advertisement and approached the man, asking if he had posted the sign. "Sure," he said. "It's the only way I can get people to stop." The sign in question offered the sale of ten-dollar bags of marijuana.

BLADDER CONTROL TO MAJOR TOM

A car pulled into the parking lot of a combination gas station and convenience store and a man jumped out of the driver's side and ran into the store. Within minutes he had accomplished his plan, to rob the place. He ran back to the car and threw open the door, tossed in the bag of money, and watched as his best friend dove out of the car urgently, needing to find a place to go to the bathroom. The criminal's cohort trotted around the convenience store looking for a private place to pee while the driver yelled at him to get back in the getaway car. The man's friend ignored him and went about his business, seemingly oblivious to the fact that the man had just committed a robbery. After several failed attempts to coax his associate back into the car, the man got in and drove away, leaving his friend at the scene of the crime. The police arrived shortly afterward and found the man's friend still wandering around the convenience store, and whistled for him to come over. The friend was very obedient and very friendly, and why not, since he was a dog. The canine cohort was content to let the police rub his belly and scratch him behind the ears. While the cops were in the vicinity of the dog's neck, they looked at his dog tags, which contained his master's name, address, and phone number. Within the day the pooch's owner was in trouble—but he didn't get sent to the doghouse . . . he got sent to the big house.

I'M READY FOR MY CLOSE-UP, MR. DEMILLE

A man who considered himself an expert safecracker broke into a small Bloomington, Indiana, business he knew kept more than $7,000 in cash. He had checked out the place previously, and since it didn't have a burglar alarm and the safe was an older model, the crook thought the heist would be a cakewalk. As he was working away at the safe, he noticed a small red light shining from the corner of the ceiling and realized immediately that it was a surveillance camera. Our safecracker thought he'd take a crack at disabling the camera instead of trying to hide his identity. He climbed up on a chair, pulled out a screwdriver from his collection of safecracking tools, and removed the camera from its brackets. He then jumped off the chair, opened the safe, and took off with both the camera and the money. The only thing the criminal forgot was that the camera was connected to a tape deck in the office—so although he got away with the camera, he left an extremely good close-up of his face on the videotape. Remember: when you focus your attention on a project, make sure something isn't focused on you.

An inmate in the Auburn Hills, Michigan, jail was able to escape and left a note bragging to the authorities. The note read, "By the time you read this, I'll be halfway to Europe." Before the day was over, the man was back in his cell, having been caught a mere three miles away.

SIGN ON THE DOTTED LINE

What is the last thing someone would do if they discovered that someone had stolen three bags of marijuana from their locker? Surely they wouldn't be stupid enough to fill out a missing-property claim, right? Well, that's just what one Welland, Ontario, man did when he returned to his locker at a St. Catharines bus terminal and found his pot missing. While he was busy filling out the form, station officials were busy calling the police. He was taken into custody after a brief struggle and charged with possession of a controlled substance, assaulting a police officer, and obstructing police work. Talk about reefer madness.

A BANK NOTE

A robber who apparently had a fear of public speaking composed a two-page holdup letter and presented it to the
teller at a Des Moines, Iowa, bank. The teller looked over the
letter and told the robber that although she knew it was a
holdup, she was having a hard time understanding the writing.
She asked if she could get another teller to help her decipher
the letter. One of the details the teller had trouble with was the
fact that the note demanded $19 trillion; that, she told the rob-
ber, would be impossible, as the bank didn't have that much
cash in the vault. The robber agreed to allow the teller to gain
the assistance of another teller to help with the letter. When the
other teller arrived, the robber said he realized that the letter
was a little convoluted, although it had taken him two weeks to
write, and that they should take their time reading it. He told
them he would wait outside while they read the letter and have
a cigarette so as not to violate bank policy by smoking inside the
lobby. He mentioned, on his way out, that if he wasn't finished
with his smoke by the time they bagged up the $19 trillion, they
could just bring it to him. The manager of the bank and the
tellers agreed that the man was probably harmless, but he had
threatened to rob the bank, so they alerted the police. In order
to stall the man, a security guard went outside to tell him that
his demands were being considered. The police arrived shortly

afterward and placed the man under arrest without incident. The only comment the robber had was, "I guess they denied my robbery request! They probably couldn't come up with the nineteen trillion. I would have settled for a hundred million!" What he did was settle for a lot less money and a lot more time.

SHARP KNIFE, DULL ROBBER

*A*n out-of-shape criminal from Sudbury, Ontario, was arrested and charged with the attempted robbery of a candy store. The easily winded robber entered the store, pulled out an X-Acto knife, and threatened the clerk with it. The clerk, unfazed by the small razor, picked up the phone and called 911 while the thief watched. When the police arrived, the box-cutter bandit was still in the store. Asked why he hadn't tried to make a break for it, the slow sneak thief replied, "I can't run too fast." The police were kind enough to give the poor man a lift–to police headquarters.

Two men in Loveland, Colorado, were arrested for robbing a pet store—for some reason they had stolen five hedgehogs.

BY ANY MEANS POSSIBLE

The owner of a Ford Probe was waiting at a traffic light when a man came out of nowhere, put a knife to his throat, demanded the car, pushed him out, and drove away. The car thief had only driven a short distance when he collided with a pickup truck, totaling the car. Now he knew he was really in trouble–not only had he stolen a car, but he was about to be guilty of a hit-and-run. The criminal quickly looked around for another mode of transportation and found a hot little pink-and-white number and took off. When the police apprehended him, he claimed he was the rightful owner of the set of wheels and was simply on his way home. The police doubted the man's explanation, because his new getaway vehicle was a little girl's bicycle. The man was caught furiously pedaling away from the scene and was charged with, among other things, two counts of larceny: one for the car and one for the bike. Look, Ma . . . no brains.

IT DOESN'T ALWAYS PAY TO ADVERTISE

An inmate at the San Mateo County, California, minimum-security jail decided he'd had enough of prison life and simply strolled away during work release. He got a little tired of walking after a while and stopped at a pay phone to call a friend to come pick him up. But try as he might, the convict couldn't remember his friend's phone number, so he called directory assistance to get it. Unfortunately, he accidentally dialed 911 instead of 411, then quickly hung up the phone when a dispatcher answered. The police sent out a cruiser to check on the 911 hang-up anyway and found the man still in the phone booth and still wearing his prison shirt, with the words PROPERTY OF SAN MATEO COUNTY HONOR CAMP written on it. "They could see it through the top of his jacket," Sheriff's lieutenant Larry Boss said. At least when they took the inmate back to celebrate his reunion with his fellow prisoners, he was already dressed for the occasion.

NEXT TIME, FOCUS YOUR ATTENTION

Two men in San Diego were arrested for burglary when a camera they had stolen turned them in. Here's what happened. The police were investigating one of the men on a separate charge and noticed a new video camera in the man's apartment. The man didn't have a receipt for the camera, and he couldn't give a believable explanation of how it had come into his possession. The police confiscated the video camera, and after they'd watched the tape, they arrested the man and his accomplice and charged them with burglary. Among the scenes on the videotape was one, shot at an extremely odd angle, showing the two men congratulating each other on a burglary well done, flaunting some of the merchandise they had stolen, and complimenting themselves on being smart enough not only to steal the video camera but also to remember to take the instruction manual. Unfortunately, the two had never read the manual and had inadvertently turned the camera on and left it on a table when they were celebrating their burglary success. Smile, you're on *Candid Camera*.

*During a picnic of county probation officers
in Yuba City, California, two thieves
failed in their attempt to steal a
barbecue grill—the grill was still hot.*

IF THE SHOE FITS

A twenty-seven-year-old woman jogged into a store with a pair of her husband's tennis shoes, asked if the clerk could repair the laces, left the shoes, told him she would be back later to pick them up, and jogged out. When the clerk examined the shoes, he noticed that something had been left in them. He reached into one shoe and miraculously pulled out several bags of marijuana. The police were called, and a subsequent search of the couple's home revealed thirty pounds of "high-grade" marijuana and dozens of weapons. My question isn't why they hid the pot in the sneaker; it's why she took the sneakers to a store to have the laces repaired!

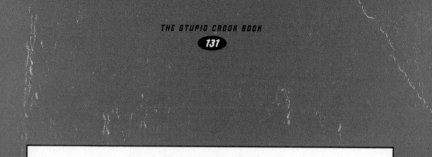

THERE'LL BE TIME ENOUGH FOR COUNTIN' WHEN THE DEALIN'S DONE

A man entered a Baltimore, Maryland, branch of Signet Bank, walked straight to the teller, and handed her a note. The note demanded money, and the teller, as trained, gave the robber the cash without any static. She then set off the silent alarm that alerts the local police station. The police always respond quickly to a bank-robbery alarm; they occasionally catch the criminal within a short distance of the bank but certainly don't expect to get there before the robber leaves. Only that's what happened in this case. You see, after the man received the money, he walked over to a nearby counter and began counting his haul. He was still in the process of tallying his take when the police took him away.

COUNTERFEIT BILL

*S*ince counterfeiters deal with altering reality, sometimes their own reality gets a little altered as well. Case in point: A counterfeiting ring in New Delhi, India, got caught when its members got greedy and looked to cash in on some fake currency. Potential buyers were apprehensive about the newly printed bills for several reasons, the first one being the denomination . . . the crooks had printed one-million-dollar bills. The second thing that alerted the customers was the enormous discount at which the counterfeiters were selling the money. The third clue they received was that the seller was supplying them with a "certificate of authenticity." And finally, the fourth reason for suspicion was that the bill had Bill on the front–Bill Clinton. I feel their pain.

A TWO-BIT DRILL THIEF

A Builders Square store in Homewood, Illinois, was busy as usual, with people shopping for merchandise to improve their homes. A man stood in the checkout line with other *Tool Time* buddies, and when it was his turn, placed an electric drill on the counter. The man reached into his wallet and pulled out a hundred-dollar bill, which the clerk ran through a counterfeit-detection device. The bill came up as being genuine, and as the clerk was putting the drill in a bag, the customer pulled out a gun and demanded all the cash in the register. The clerk quickly obliged and handed the man the entire contents–ninety-five dollars. The man took the money and left the store. Sounds like a successful robbery, right? Well, it would have been if the man hadn't left both his original hundred-dollar bill and the drill on the counter. I wonder if the clerk was allowed to keep the five dollars as a tip?

A man in Wilmington, North Carolina, was arrested and charged with theft after he dug up and stole fifteen hundred Venus flytraps.

SMALL-CHANGE ARTIST

*T*he police in Corpus Christi, Texas, think they've finally found the man responsible for a string of gumball-machine thefts in the area, after the suspect's landlord tipped off the authorities to the man's whereabouts. The landlord became suspicious of the man when he went to his apartment to collect the rent and saw a massive pile of jawbreakers on the floor. But what really clued the landlord in was the fact that the man routinely paid his weekly rent entirely in quarters. Gives a whole new meaning to the phrase "living quarters."

During a police lineup, the detective told each man to step forward and repeat the threat delivered at the robbery: "Give me all your money or I'll shoot." One man stepped out of line and yelled, "That's not what I said!"

YOU PUT YOUR LEFT FOOT IN, YOU TAKE YOUR LEFT FOOT OUT . . .

*U*sually escape plans are hatched by a team of prisoners who work in tandem to pull off their self-awarded release program. But one convict in the Henry County, Georgia, jail masterminded this prison escape on his own. Using a gun he had smuggled into his cell, he was able to get the drop on four guards. He ushered them into his cell and locked the door. Slowly creeping down the hall with the loaded weapon, he thought he was home free. But he'd overlooked the fact that all prison guards carry walkie-talkies, and that's what they used to inform the front-desk guards of an unwanted (or wanted) visitor. Having added attempted escape to his charges, our quickly caught con will be a visitor to the jail for a long time now.

NO DEPOSIT, NO RETURN

A man with a neat military haircut marched into the Fort Belvoir Federal Credit Union and stood in line for the next teller. One of the tellers thought she recognized the young man and signaled him to come to her window. The man politely asked the teller if she would wire $2,900 to his home in Texas and also gave her a large pile of money to be deposited into his account. "It couldn't be him," she must have thought to herself as she went into the back room with the money. Acting on a hunch, she decided to check the serial numbers on the top two five-dollars bills. The bills matched those of the $4,759 that had been taken in a robbery twelve days earlier. That's where she had seen the young man before–standing in front of her nearly two weeks ago, without a mask, robbing the bank. She called the police. When the military police arrived, they were surprised to find one of their own accused of robbing the bank and then trying to deposit the money he'd stolen back into his account–a man who, as a private in the military police, had undergone FBI training on handling bank robberies. I guess he was trained in the proper way of halting a bank robbery, not conducting one.

TAKEN FOR A RIDE

The man's eyes darted around the bank as he reached into his pocket and pulled out the crumpled holdup note. The teller at the Canadian Imperial Bank of Commerce in Gatineau, Quebec, accepted the note, unfolded it, but wasn't able to read it. The note was written in English, and the teller only understood French. She left the robber standing there and took the note to some other tellers for assistance. The man began to feel uneasy as a crowd gathered around the teller to help her translate the note. Panic got the best of him, and he dashed out of the bank into his getaway car–a taxi he had waiting around the corner. He gave the driver instructions to take him across the river to downtown Ottawa and sat back in the cab to calm his nerves. Once in the city, the man thought he would be able to go through with the robbery again and told the driver to turn the car around and head back to Gatineau. The driver looked at the haggard man sitting in the backseat and asked if he had enough money to pay the fare. Checking his pockets, the man admitted that he was short of cash and couldn't pay the meter. The driver slammed on the brakes, got out of his car, and called the police. The man was arrested and charged with armed robbery in connection with the failed attempt at the bank. He was later charged with a second count of armed robbery involving a Bank of Nova Scotia in Gatineau. Said Sergeant Richard Longpre of the Gatineau Police Department, "It wasn't such a smooth job by that guy."

TIMING IS EVERYTHING

*T*iming is of the utmost importance when one is attempting to rob a bank. Timing to hit the bank when it has the most money in its vaults, timing between the accomplices, and timing of the getaway are all crucial elements of a successful bank robbery. One of the most critical elements of time, however, is making sure the bank is open in the first place. "They just made mistakes in their times," said holdup squad detective Mike Earl. "Usually they plan a little better. But that's how we catch these guys . . . some of them are pretty stupid." Detective Earl was talking about an attempted bank robbery of the Bank of Nova Scotia in Toronto. Four men whose intention it was to rob the bank ran to the glass doors, grabbed the door handles, and pulled–nothing happened. The bank hadn't opened for business yet. The tellers inside were startled by the four men furiously pulling at the locked doors and quickly alerted the police. The men looked at their watches, looked at each other in disgust, jumped back into their black Honda, and left. They were, for all practical purposes, robbers ahead of their time.

THE SEVEN OOPS

*I*t was a yet-to-be-solved crime wave in Albany, Georgia: three bank robberies and three business robberies all attributed to seven criminal cohorts. An anonymous tip led the police to a residence that turned into a gold mine—all seven of the suspected robbers lived there. When confronted with the evidence the police had gathered against them and after a few short minutes of questioning, the seven confessed to the string of robberies. Even if they hadn't confessed to the crimes, they had already framed themselves—literally. One of the criminals was an amateur photographer and had taken photos of every robbery they had committed. The photographs were enlarged and proudly displayed on the walls for everyone to see—even the police. The next time they were in front of a camera was for their mug shots.

WHAT GOES UP MUST COME DOWN

*I*n police jargon, a criminal's MO means his modus operandi (method of operating)–basically, a pattern one routinely follows when conducting a crime. But in this case this criminal's MO should stand for "mostly obtuse." Here's the sequence of events that led to this man's fortunate (for him) capture. First, the thief cut his hand badly when he broke through the roof of a liquor store in San Antonio, Texas. He jumped down through the hole but soon realized that he didn't know how to hoist the stolen liquor up through the opening in the roof. He picked up a bottle of whiskey, took careful aim, and tossed the bottle toward the opening. The bottle missed the hole, smashed to the ground, and set off the burglar alarm. The burglar (I even hate to use that word) slipped on the spilled liquor, fell to the floor, and cut himself on the broken glass. As he was scrambling, empty-handed, back through the hole in the ceiling, his wallet fell out of his pocket and landed on the floor. Once on the roof, our thwarted thief took in a deep breath of fresh air, turned around, and fell off the roof. He limped away, battered, beaten, and bleeding, and left an easy-to-follow crimson trail of blood from the crime scene to his house–less than a block from the store.

NOT A GOOD HUMOR MAN

*T*he police in Potomac, Maryland, in response to a call about a home burglary, were patrolling the area around the crime scene. They noticed a man sitting in a car and watched as he threw a Popsicle stick out of the window and onto the road, unwrapped another Popsicle, and put it in his mouth. Two officers got out of their patrol car and approached the man and soon had him under arrest. Was he arrested for littering? Nope. He was arrested for the burglary. The police knew they had the right man, as the only thing stolen during the robbery was a box of Popsicles.

A ROSE BY ANY OTHER NAME . . .

*T*he editorial page of a local newspaper offers an excellent opportunity for one to speak one's mind about issues of concern. One such letter that appeared in the *Kingsport (Tennessee) Times-News* was focused on exposing conditions in local jails. Drafted by inmate Travis Nelms, who had been incarcerated nine times in three years, the letter read, in part, "We the inmates here at the Sullivan County Jail [are] concerned that here we all [are] treated as criminals." I guess you can't blame the guy for trying to write a wrong.

YOU CAN'T WIN 'EM ALL

A man called 911 reporting that he had just been robbed of over $2,000 in cash. The police were dispatched, and they found the man beaten and bruised and very angry. It took the police only a few minutes to get there because they had just previously been summoned to respond to a bank robbery in the same exact area. The robbery victim quickly approached the patrol car and angrily explained to them what had happened. He admitted he was the man who'd robbed the bank. But the real crime, to his mind, was the fact that someone saw him rob the bank, jumped him, beat him up, and took the stolen money. The battered bank robber demanded that the police find the man who'd mugged him and gave them a very good description of the perpetrator. The mugger was never found, but the empty-handed (and empty-headed) bank robber was sentenced to a rather long stretch in the county pen.

GETTING A LEG UP ON CRIME

A man who robbed a St. Louis grocery store, to avoid being identified, had made sure he was carrying a spare shirt in his back pocket. In the process of changing on the run, however, the robber forgot that he had also placed his gun in the same pocket.

When he reached for the shirt, he hit the trigger of the gun and shot himself in the leg. It wasn't long before the police found the bleeding robber in the backseat of a car just two blocks from the grocery store, passed out from the excruciating pain. He was placed in custody and rushed to the hospital. He survived his injury and was later convicted of the robbery. During his getaway, the guy had probably thought he was a fast runner–but not faster than a speeding bullet.

GUNS DON'T KILL PEOPLE— BULLETS DO!

*T*here are ill-equipped criminals, and then there are mentally ill-equipped criminals; the latter is where this would-be robber obviously belongs. We've all made mistakes, and some of the stories in this book illustrate an error in judgment or lack of a plan on some level or another—but this guy got everything wrong. First he chose as his target of robbery H&J Leather & Firearms—a gun shop (i.e., a place where they keep a lot of guns). His second mistake was not realizing that a large number of the adult population is licensed to carry concealed handguns in the area he chose to rob (i.e., the store that has lots of guns also has lots of people with guns). Another error was that he didn't notice a marked King County police car in the parking lot—even though he had to walk around it to get in the front door. And then he didn't grasp the full effect of seeing the police officer in full uniform standing next to the counter drinking a cup of coffee. The robber pulled out his handgun, fired off a few warning shots, and announced he was holding up the place. The clerk and the police officer returned fire—extremely accurate fire, I must add—and the criminal's career was over before it had begun.

FRIED, STEWED, OR BAKED?

*N*otorious criminals are given nicknames that match their heinous crimes: the Boston Strangler, Jack the Ripper, Son of Sam, and the Zucchini Bandit. Yep, the Zucchini Bandit. But we won't have to worry about this vegetable for a long time, as he was sentenced to eighteen years to life in prison. Justice Randall Eng, who sentenced the man, declared, "You added to the climate of fear we have to live in." His crime? He held up a man and took twenty dollars and a watch, claiming that he had a concealed weapon in his coat—but the weapon turned out to be a zucchini. The victim probably wondered if the man really had a gun in his pocket or if he was just glad to see him.

An Atlanta man who was serving as a member of a jury was arrested when he took his one-hour lunch break during the trial and went to the suburbs to buy drugs.

A CRIME MOST FOUL

A police officer in Perth, Western Australia, pulled over a man who was speeding and watched as he popped something into his mouth. Immediately the officer suspected that the man was getting rid of some evidence, probably drugs, and approached the car. The patrolman knocked on the man's window, and the driver slowly rolled it down and asked the officer what the problem might be. That's when the smell almost knocked the policeman down. Was it the smell of pot? Nope. The man had deliberately chewed a clove of fresh garlic in anticipation of the policeman's approach. Once the officer caught his breath, he informed the man of his rights and placed him under arrest. During the man's trial, the judge enacted a seldom-used Australian law that defines assault as "the direct or indirect application of force, including gas or odor, in such a manner as to cause personal discomfort." The malodorous malefactor was fined, and the whole courtroom breathed a sigh of relief.

THE EYES HAVE IT

The police in El Cerrito, California, responded quickly to a report of "shots fired" at a local apartment complex. Paramedics on the scene helped a twenty-eight-year-old man who'd been wounded by two gunmen after they'd struggled during an argument and he'd been shot. Detectives thoroughly searched the residence for clues and finally found one staring them right in the face—it was a plastic eyeball marked "A. Harris." The wounded man wasn't named Harris and, anyway, he had both of his eyes, so the police deduced that the eyeball was an eye-witness piece of evidence against one of the shooters. The primary suspect in this case was a man who lost his left eye in a shotgun-related accident years ago and whose first name started with an *A* and last name was Harris. I guess when Harris's partner told him to keep an eye out for the police, he took him literally.

PUSH ME, PULL YOU

A number of bank robberies are hampered because of holdup notes that include the robber's name and phone number, the lack of a weapon, an ineffective disguise, and the like, and usually these robbers don't make it out the door. But in the case of one aspiring bank robber, he didn't even make it in the door. Employees of the Durham, North Carolina, Federal Savings Bank became frightened when they saw a man in a sweatshirt with the hood pulled tightly over his face pounding loudly on the front door. Why couldn't he get in—was the door locked? Nope. The man was trying to push the door open, not having noticed the PULL sign above the handle. The unidentified man was linked to another attempted robbery in Durham. Yep, you guessed it—same MO. The crook failed at that robbery attempt, too, when he again attempted to push open a pull door. The pushy robber probably attributed his failure to a loose hinge on the door. (Insert your own loose-hinge joke here.)

THIS CRIME WAS A REAL RIB STICKER

A thief was chilled to the bone after getting trapped in the freezer of a Longhorn Barbecue Restaurant in Spokane, Washington. The frozen felon had accidentally let the freezer door close behind him when he went in to purloin some sirloin. When the sheriff's deputies thawed the thief, they noticed that he was completely covered in barbecue sauce. The man had been hugging huge racks of still-warm barbecued ribs as his only source of heat.

Thieves in Jonesboro, Arkansas, robbed several restaurants in the area—stealing an estimated eight thousand pounds of grease.

SORRY, WRONG NUMBER

*T*his is a story of a criminal who really had a bright idea; unfortunately, he was a dim bulb. A man in Aiken, South Carolina, was sentenced to two months in prison and fined for stealing a car. His plan was to eliminate the car's VIN (vehicle identification number)—it's that long string of numbers on a metal plate visible through the car's front windshield. He successfully obliterated the number but knew he had to replace the number with a bogus one so as not to arouse suspicion. The number the man chose was his downfall—it didn't match the numerical sequencing of a VIN, and besides, it was his own social security number.

A STRIKE, A SPLIT, AND NO BRAINS TO SPARE

A "smash-and-grab" robbery is pretty much what it sounds like. A fast-thinking criminal who suddenly sees something that strikes his fancy will pick up a heavy object (cinder block, large rock, sewer lid, and so on), "smash" the window, and "grab" the stuff he wants. Not the type of material that cat burglar stories are made of—but a crime that takes place quite often nonetheless. The heavy object of choice in this particular smash-and-grab in Waynesboro, Virginia, was a bowling ball. The police quickly and easily apprehended the man and his three juvenile accomplices because they left the bowling ball at the scene; and the bowling ball had one of their names engraved on it. These guys went from playing tenpin to serving ten in the pen.

DOWN THE DRAIN

*T*wo men were arrested in Clayton, Missouri, thus ending a crime spree that had struck several houses in the area. The burglars would methodically remove the copper gutters and drain spouts from the houses and then sell the copper for scrap. The boys must have really loved their work, because even though it took them several hours to remove the hardware from each house, it only netted them eight to ten dollars' worth of salable scrap. And people say most criminals are lazy!

The Understatement of the Year:
A man who robbed a retail store in Belton,
Missouri, lost most of the stolen money during
his getaway. He admitted to the police after
his arrest, "I'm just a novice robber."

URINE TROUBLE NOW!

A van in Coventry, England, was broken into, and the crooks
made off with two cases of wine and two cases of a bottled
product called Silent Roar. Since the wine and the other product
were in the same van, the unsuspecting thieves might have
thought Silent Roar to be some kind of powerful alcohol. "If they
don't know what Silent Roar is, they might end up drinking the
lot," said a police officer investigating the break-in. The product
is used to keep cats out of gardens; its main ingredient is lion's
urine. So if the crooks drank the stuff, there would have been a
roar, all right, but I don't think it would have been silent!

PAY TO THE ORDER OF . . .

A woman walked into a Durham, North Carolina, bank to cash a check. A simple matter, right? Well, not if your brain is composed of simple matter. The woman in question tried to cash a check that wasn't made out to her; in fact, it wasn't made out to a person. The check was made out to the Tension Envelope Company, and the woman claimed to be Mrs. Tension Envelope. The teller didn't believe her and summoned the police. If she thought tension was in her name before trying to cash the check, I wonder how she felt afterward.

A similar check-cashing attempt occurred years earlier when a man handed a teller a company check and claimed the check was made out to him:
Mr. Roadway V. Express.

JAILHOUSE ROCK

*T*his convenience-store robber seemed to be doing everything right: he had a weapon, he had a mask (which he was wearing), and he had successfully held up a Charlotte, North Carolina, 7-Eleven and was on his way out. The man had chosen an Elvis Presley mask to wear to the holdup, and after he got the money, in his hands must have gotten "all shook up." He turned his head so quickly as he spun around to make his escape that the mask stayed in place and didn't twist with his head. The clerk watched as the joker disguised as the King, who was wearing the King mask backward now, slammed headfirst into the door frame and knocked himself unconscious. When the police arrived to arrest the sleeping King, they must have felt like singing, "Going to a party in the county jail . . . "

PAPER OR PLASTIC?

A man wearing a paper bag over his head entered Charlie's Supermarket in Jacksonville, Florida, with the intention of robbing the store. However, during the holdup, the bag shifted and the sacked suspect was unable to see. In his panic he demanded, "Give me the register." But since the robber was speaking from inside a bag, the clerk had a hard time understanding the demand. The bandit attempted to create another mouth hole, but he became overzealous and the entire bag split open, exposing his face. "Bob!" the clerk exclaimed, knowing him as a regular in the store, as the thief high-tailed it out the door. When detectives questioned the clerk about whether he thought Bob was armed or not, the clerk couldn't give a definitive answer—you see, Bob had put a paper bag over his hand, too. No word on whether the paper bags were from that store or the competition's.

THE DEAL OF THE CENTURY

Drug deals usually go down in the blink of an eye: a quick exchange of money for drugs usually concealed in a handshake or passed by some other covert manner. In most cases dealers work on a cash-only basis–but one dealer from Oneida, New York, didn't want to pass up a $1,500 deal and decided to go ahead and take a check. When the pusher pushed the check through the bank teller's window, she told him she wouldn't be able to cash the check since it was drawn on an out-of-state bank, and the man didn't have an account anyway. Afraid of being ripped off, the dealer did the only thing he could think of–he contacted the police and told them the whole story. He must have thought the police would track down the buyer and squeeze the $1,500 out of him; what they did, however, was squeeze the pusher behind bars.

A man who was arrested for stealing $10,000 worth of equipment from a Rolling Meadows, Illinois, museum and theater confessed, "I'm not a very good burglar. I'm still trying to come to terms with my own stupidity."

LET'S SEE WHAT DEVELOPS

A motorist in Bern, Switzerland, was speeding along when he noticed one of the newly installed cameras that automatically photograph traffic violators. The man knew he would be in trouble if the photograph ever got back to the police, so he turned his car around and went back to where the camera was located. He unlocked his trunk, pulled out some tools, and began dismantling the device. While his full attention was on removing the camera, the full attention of the police was focused on him. The officers had driven by and realized what the man was doing. He was arrested and charged with both speeding and attempted robbery. The next photograph taken of the man was at police headquarters.

HORNING IN ON

Knowing that the horn of the rhinoceros was a valuable commodity on the black market, a Tokyo man hatched a brilliant scheme. If ground up and placed in small packets, a single rhino horn could fetch several thousand yen because of its properties as a powerful aphrodisiac. He broke into a Tokyo museum and quickly located the stuffed rhinoceros on display. Working with amazing dexterity, the burglar removed the horn from the rhino and made his escape without incident. It might have been that he was working in the dark (or that the man kept his mind in the dark), or maybe he was too engrossed in what he was doing and wasn't paying attention. Whatever the reason, our blind burglar didn't notice the huge sign hanging over the stuffed rhinoceros, which explained that the valuable rhino horn . . . had been replaced by a fake plastic one. The man thought he was stealing the horn of plenty, but he wound up getting the shaft.

ARRESTED IN THIRTY MINUTES OR LESS

A deliveryman working for Papa John's Pizza was surprised by two men who robbed him of thirty dollars, two pizzas, and a soda. He reported the incident to the police, and the perpetrators were quickly apprehended. Where was the slipup in this robbery scenario? Simple. The robbers forgot that only thirty minutes before, they had given Papa John's their address when they'd ordered the pizzas and the soft drink. To make sure they had the right men, the police, once they were in the apartment, pushed the redial button on the crook's phone–"Good afternoon, Papa John's" was the answer on the other end of the line. That was the end of the line for these two thick-crust thieves.

A burglar who was watching his four-year-old daughter broke into a Newark, New Jersey, home, stole several items, and successfully got away, leaving only one small clue— his four-year-old daughter.

SEE NO EVIL

A man was arrested in the parking lot of the Old Kent Bank in Grand Haven, Michigan, shortly after he had robbed the place. The bank robber was shortsighted in his robbery scheme because he was . . . well, shortsighted. After the man robbed the bank, he informed the teller that he was visually impaired and needed assistance in exiting the bank. Of course he didn't see the teller push the silent alarm button before slowly . . . very slowly . . . leading the man out the front door and into the waiting arms of the police. A robbery like that must have been a sight to see.

BUTTON, BUTTON, WHO'S GOT THE BUTTON?

*H*ere's the case of a twenty-five-year-old would-be robber who turned himself in at the scene of the crime–by accident. The man made several mistakes in his attempt to hold up a 7-Eleven in Shoreline, Washington, one of which was the wearing of a black ski mask– perched on top of his head, not over his face. He then couldn't figure out how to work the cash register and was unable to open it. And finally, during his frantic button-pushing marathon, he accidentally triggered the silent alarm, which brought the police to the store and him to jail. An excellent example of cutting out the middleman.

"I" BEFORE "E" EXCEPT AFTER "C"

*T*he police in Clay, New York, were hot on the trail of two suspects who had masterminded a small-time counterfeiting ring printing fake raffle tickets. The raffle tickets in question were sold for two dollars each, and the proceeds apparently were used to fund the criminals' cigarette-smoking habits. It turned out our two felons were high school sophomores who printed the bogus raffle tickets on a home computer. They apparently forgot to use the spell-check function on the computer, since they were discovered because the word *raffle* was misspelled.

A man who was suspected of burglarizing a Beverly Hills, California, home was frantically running away from the police. He turned to see how much distance there was between himself and the officers and slammed into a low-hanging tree branch, knocking himself unconscious.

A BAD WAY TO AVOID A LATE CHARGE

A branch of the Austin National Bank, in Texas, had been robbed earlier in the day, and the police were combing the area looking for clues as to the whereabouts of the robber. An hour after the robbery a report came through to police headquarters that the money from the heist had been recovered and an arrest was imminent. Apparently the bank robber had taken a rental car to the robbery to use as his getaway car–but in his haste to return the car and get away himself, he'd left all the money in the backseat. Why would a man, after a successful bank heist, be in such a hurry to return a rental car that he would leave all the money in it? According to a sheriff's spokesman, "I guess he didn't want to get charged for another day." Believe me, he'll be charged for more than another day now.

LET'S PLAY COPS AND ROBBERS

We're all kids at heart, even if that heart beats in a burglar. A Detroit man who had scoped out a house struck while the owners were away, allowing him plenty of time to clean out their home. He had done a very thorough job, and on the way out he saw something that must have caught his eye. Was it an overlooked piece of jewelry? A rare coin? A hidden shotgun? Nope. It was a blob of Silly Putty sitting on the desk in one of the children's rooms. The burglar picked up the putty and started playing with it. After he had amused himself, he put it back on the desk, loaded up his car with the family's belongings, and drove away. Investigators on the scene discovered the fingered Silly Putty and sent it to the lab for fingerprint analysis–and they found a match. Soon they arrested a man who had recently been released from jail after serving time for five previous burglaries.

WATCH WHAT YOU'RE DOING

*T*om Burgess, a clerk at a San Diego convenience store, thought nothing of the customer who entered his store, went over to the coffee machine, poured himself a cup to go, and wandered back to the counter. The man pulled out his wallet and set it on the counter to pay for the coffee and then, surprisingly, demanded everything in the cash register. The robber was disappointed when Burgess told him there was no money in the register. Not wanting to leave empty-handed, the thief stole the clerk's wristwatch and quickly left the store with the coffee. After Burgess called the police, he was surprised when he saw that, in his haste, the thief had left his wallet on the counter, complete with social security card and California driver's license. "Not very bright," explained Burgess. The criminal won't have time to enjoy his watch, as he'll be serving time and being watched.

Leonardo's Pizza in Akron, Ohio, narrowly
escaped being robbed because the gunman slipped
on a patch of grease from a pizza dropped earlier
in the evening, hit the floor, and knocked
himself unconscious.

WHAT TEN-LETTER TERM STARTS WITH GAS?

*I*t seems that a robber decided to strike a downtown Seattle bank and selected as his getaway car a hired Graytop Cab. He told the driver to drop him off and wait for him, as he would only be a minute or two. The driver had recently received an expensive parking ticket in that area and decided to pull around to the side of the building and wait for his customer there. The robber stormed out of the bank and stopped dead in his tracks when he noticed he was lacking the hack. The cabdriver watched as his fare ran down the street followed by several police cars. The robber managed to escape this time, but he'd left a nylon bag in the cab that contained some of his belongings. As the police were questioning the cabdriver, they noticed that the meter was still running–and apparently so was the bank robber. The bank robber's career finally ran out of gas when he was apprehended after his fourth alleged bank robbery in Seattle. The bank robber successfully robbed the bank, jumped into his getaway car, and sped off (he didn't use a cab this time). Unfortunately, the gas tank was about as empty as this guy's head, and he was spotted twenty miles from the bank, filling up at a local BP station.

WE'RE LOOKING FOR
A FEW GOOD MEN

*A*n army sergeant in La Junta, Colorado, who was
behind on his monthly quota of prospective recruits—I
guess he wasn't doing more by 7:00 A.M. than most of us
do all day—was arrested and charged with burglary. In
order to get more men to "be all that they can be," he
broke into the navy recruiting station next door and stole
prospective enrollees' files.

Burglars using a welding torch to break open a safe in Rich's Department Store in Salem, Massachusetts, turned the flame up too high. The money inside burst into flame, and the resulting smoke set off the store's fire alarm.

ROB THEM UNTIL YOU'RE BLUE IN THE FACE

*T*he usual weapon of choice for a convenience-store robbery is either a handgun, a shotgun, or a knife–but this criminal's unique weapon was truly a breath of fresh air. The would-be robber walked up to the clerk of an Albuquerque, New Mexico, convenience store and said that if she didn't surrender all the cash, he would hold his breath until he passed out. Then, he claimed, he would sue the store, which would be responsible for his injuries on its property. The clerk looked at the man a minute and then broke out laughing. The windless robber kept his promise and held his breath–gradually turning red. A quick exhalation and a gasp for oxygen made the crook and the clerk realize that the threat was just hot air. The crook fled from the store and ran straight into an off-duty police officer who had stopped by for coffee. A convenient arrest for an inconvenient convenience-store robber.

TO TELL THE TRUTH

*W*e've all seen episodes of *Perry Mason* where the guilty
party, perched on the witness stand, finally confesses to
the crime under Mason's battering cross-examination. Perry
smiles confidently, Hamilton Burger shakes his head in disgust,
Della gives Perry a coy and slightly flirtatious smile, and Paul
Drake slaps him on the back and lights up a cigarette. In most
cases, however, criminal confessions aren't this dramatic. Case in
point: St. Louis, Missouri, police officers arrived on the scene of
a possible burglary in progress and found one suspect there.
When the police asked what the man was doing, he stated, "A
burglary, I guess." Soon the man's accomplice was noticed exiting the back of the building with a vacuum cleaner, and he was
asked the same question. He responded honestly and quickly,
"Burglarizing the place." Your honor, I rest my case.

A HEAVY-DUTY CRIMINAL

A number of criminals accidentally leave a trail of clues that
the police and detectives use to track them down. Clues for
crime-scene investigators like fingerprints, hair samples, and
footprints are all crucial elements in uncovering the whereabouts
and identification of a criminal. But in the case of one seventeen-
year-old, four-hundred-pound burglar near San Antonio, Texas,
the police were immediately hot on his trail—because he left
behind a trail of discarded ice-cream wrappers. The overweight
underachiever had broken into a residence and raided the refrigerator, stealing a box of ice-cream sandwiches and devouring
the treats on his way home—which was within walking distance—or should I say waddling distance?

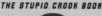
Burglars broke into a Dallas, Texas, bird sanctuary and stole twenty-five homing pigeons—which, according to the birds' trainer, didn't make any sense, as the birds, once out of their cages, would instinctively return to the sanctuary.

A CRIME THAT WENT TO THEIR HEADS

*T*wo Argentine men went into a local hamburger restaurant in the northern Argentine city of Resistencia and asked the manager if they could use the toilet. Once inside the bathroom the two men wrenched the toilet off its moorings and ran out of the restaurant. They hopped onto their waiting getaway vehicle, a motor-powered scooter, and sped down the street. The police soon apprehended them; the toilet was put back in its rightful place, and the boys were put in their place . . . the local jail. During questioning, neither suspect said why they'd wanted the toilet so badly.

NO CURSING IN THE COURTROOM

A man from Pineville, Louisiana, pleaded guilty to charges of battery and was in front of the judge to hear the terms of his probation. Before Judge Joel Chaisson began his explanation, he ordered the man to remove the voodoo curse that he had placed on the judge during his sentencing.

A man was arrested for burglary after he was caught inside a Martinsville, Indiana, home. The thief was discovered when he began playing the owners' piano at 3:00 A.M., and he didn't stop until the police arrived.

SIGN ON THE DOTTED LINE

A man in Brunswick, Georgia, walked up to a cashier at a local supermarket and presented her with a payroll check that he wished to cash. Little did she know that the payroll check was stolen—she also didn't know she was dealing with a moron. She asked the man to endorse the back of the check before she cashed it, and he quickly obliged. She gave him the cash, and the man left the store. The stolen check and the man who'd stolen it were easily tracked down because (you guessed it) he had signed his real name on the back and even included both his driver's license number and his phone number. The courts in our country work on a system of checks and balances—and when you're unbalanced, you get checked off the list.

CADDY LACK OF INTELLIGENCE

A Miami, Florida, bank robber must have considered himself a first-class criminal and decided he deserved first-class accommodations. He thought it would best suit his status to rent a limousine. Not a very odd thing to do, of course, until you realize that he rented the limo to take him to his next bank robbery. The driver took the man to a local bank but noticed that he was acting suspiciously; his suspicions were confirmed when he saw the man pull a gun out of his pants before entering the bank. The limo driver quickly called the police, and when the man exited the bank with the loot, he found a different car waiting for him–a police car. He went from riding in a stretch limo to serving a stretch of time in limbo.

A man was charged with attempted burglary and breaking and entering after he was discovered by a home owner trying to gain access to the home—the burglar had attempted to squeeze through the dog door but had gotten stuck.

YOU'D BETTER WATCH OUT!

It was a bustling antique show in Miami, Florida, and exhibitors were proudly displaying their rare and hard-to-find merchandise. One man walked up to a booth and, looking over the fine, quality antique jewelry, decided the best bargain he could get on a $3,200 watch was to slip it into his pocket without paying for it. The robber must have kept his eye only on the antiques and not the people selling them or he wouldn't have made a crucial mistake the next day. He chose an antique store at random in which to sell the watch and entered excitedly, eager to turn time into money. A woman in the store was wound tight when she saw him enter and screamed that he was the thief who had stolen her watch. She and several customers held the man until the police arrived—in the nick of time, of course. The woman who owned the watch watched as the thief who had stolen the watch was arrested by the cops on the watch.

TAKING A SHINE TO CRIME

A man obsessed with shining his shoes (a compulsion he gave in to several times a day) was arrested and convicted of burglarizing a home in Roanoke, Virginia. The forty-year-old shoeshine robber even carried his own tin of polish and a cloth with him just in case he got the urge to polish up while he was polishing off someone's belongings. But this buffing burglar glossed over two little blemishes during his last break-in: he left his personalized shoeshine rag and tin of polish (complete with fingerprints) at the scene. Prison might not be the best place for a man who likes to bend over and polish his shoes, if you know what I mean.

JUST DO IT!

*I*n some cases a criminal will return to the scene of the crime out of curiosity or to privately gloat about his clever escape. But in Memphis, Tennessee, one man returned to the scene of the crime (a home burglary) for a completely different reason. Several hours after he'd robbed a home, the burglar knocked on the door and nonchalantly asked the home owners, "I was wondering, have you-all seen my shoes? They are red-and-white Nikes." After the robber "just did it," he had sneaked off without his sneakers.

Authorities at the Blue Ridge Community work-release facility in Taylors, South Carolina, weren't overly concerned when one of their inmates escaped—because they knew the way the man thought. A week later the convict returned to the facility on his own volition, in order to claim his paycheck.

STRANGE BEDSIDE MANNER

Albuquerque, New Mexico, sheriff's deputies were searching an apartment, looking for an eighteen-year-old suspect who was wanted on probation violations stemming from a drug charge. A search of the bedroom found the suspect hiding under the bed, and when they pulled him out, his first words weren't "Okay, you found me" but "Are you here about the accident?" Not sure what the man meant, the officers questioned him about his statement and soon arrested him–not for the parole violation, however, but for being the driver of a stolen vehicle that, only a week before, had crashed into another car during a high-speed police chase and resulted in the death of two people. Had it not been for the man's bedside confession, the police admitted, the man would probably never have been caught. The penance for his confession was more than just a few Hail Marys or Our Fathers–it resulted in an extended sentence in jail.

EATING DISORDER

*T*aking the slogan "All you can eat" to its extreme, a forty-six-year-old Japanese man ate in a booth at the Royal Host Restaurant for three consecutive days. The twenty-four-hour restaurant had no choice but to continue serving the man, who eventually wound up ordering twenty dishes worth a total of $125 from early Friday through Sunday morning. According to the newspaper *Asahi,* the manager of the restaurant said the man broke no rules by sitting quietly in his booth and eating–even though his staff thought the man's refusal to leave was "weird." The man was arrested, according to Masahiro Furiya, a police spokesman in Kofu, after he tried to sneak out of the restaurant without paying when two other customers got into an argument. Our ravenous rapscallion will now be enjoying the cuisine at the local jail.

VICTIMS OF THEIR OWN CRIMES

*T*hree young men entered the Food Spot Grocery Store and started comparison shopping for bottles of iced tea. One of the men complained to the clerk that the Country Time, at seventy-five cents a bottle, was too expensive. The clerk recommended a cheaper brand, and one of the young men placed a carton on the counter. Suddenly, all three pulled out guns, pointed them at the clerk, and forced him to lie on the floor. The clerk heard the three robbers fumbling with the cash register and then tensed with fear as he heard a shot fired directly over his head. The thought of being shot to death entered the clerk's mind when he heard another shot fired. "I've had robbers shoot themselves before, but I never had two robbers shoot each other," Metro-Dade robbery detective Tom Pellechio said. Apparently one of the robbers, while reaching over the counter to open the cash register, accidentally discharged his weapon, hitting one of his accomplices in the thigh. The startled, wounded robber stepped backward and tripped over the third robber, reflexively firing his own gun and striking the first robber through both hands and the right leg. The two limping bandits and their cohort emptied the cash register and made off with about $200. They got into their car and the designated driver (the one without any bullet holes in him) drove away. The driver took his bleeding buddies to a nearby hospital, dropped them off at the emergency room door, and drove off with the guns and the money–never to be heard from again. "It was a real simple case to solve," Pellechio said. "All we had to do was drive to the hospital."

LOOSE LIPS SINK DRIPS

*I*t was a well-planned escape, and everything was going right for the Valdosta, Georgia, prisoner. He not only got out of jail, he also got out of the state—fleeing from Georgia to California. He was feeling pretty cocky and decided to buy a self-congratulatory drink and toast his superior criminal skills. After several drinks, our criminal who'd escaped the slammer was getting slammed, and he started loosening up; the loosest part of him was his tongue. He bragged loudly to anyone who came within earshot that he was too smart to be held by any jail. He got more and more inebriated and more and more vocal about escaping from jail. After passing several hours of doing shots and shooting off his mouth, the man finally passed out at the bar—that's when the annoyed bartender called the police. Since the man was intoxicated, the police volunteered to be his designated driver, with his destination being the local jail.

A DOLLAR'S NOT WORTH WHAT IT USED TO BE

A man was arrested at a hotel in Wichita, Kansas, for trying to pass counterfeit currency. Not the most stunning crime ever reported and certainly not one that merits mention in this book—except for one small detail. The confused counterfeiter was attempting to use freshly printed sixteen-dollar bills. Let's give him the benefit of the doubt: maybe they were 14.95-dollar bills and he was kind enough to include sales tax.

A shopkeeper in Norwich, Ontario, was robbed by a man armed with a bottle of toilet cleaner.

A NOTE OF RECOGNITION

A man in Salt Lake City, Utah, was loitering and acting suspicious, so two police officers approached him and asked for identification. The man reached into his pocket and absentmindedly handed them something he had used before as a form of identification. The police arrested him on the spot. What did the man give the officers? It was a holdup note the man had used in two recent robberies.

ARRESTED DEVELOPMENT

A twenty-seven-year-old man was arrested and charged with robbing a convenience store in Lancaster, Pennsylvania. How was he caught? The police watched the surveillance video and easily identified the perpetrator, as he was wearing a basketball jersey with the name of his team, Public Enemy; his team number, 6; and, of course, his last name boldly displayed on the back.

Two men who were charged with murder and armed robbery in Boynton Beach, Florida, cited as their motive the need to raise money to attend the police academy.

THE GODS MUST BE CRAZY

*I*s there a jail strong enough to hold God? It's not really a theological question—and the answer is yes. Ubiquitous Perpetuity God, who used to go by the less ostentatious name of Enrique Silberg, was arrested for exposing himself at a coffee shop and sentenced to nine months in jail. However, the sentencing judge said that God could be released to a mental-health facility if one agreed to admit him. If God were admitted to a psychiatric hospital, it would certainly make the patients with delusions of grandeur feel pretty foolish.

A PICTURE IS WORTH A THOUSAND WORDS

St. Louis circuit judge Sherri Sullivan sentenced a man to pro-bation for mailing nude photographs of himself to a nurse. When the man's probationary period ended, the judge found a letter in her mailbox with the man's return address. Maybe it was a letter apologizing for his actions, telling her that the pro-bation had made him see the error of his ways and saying that thanks to her stern yet forgiving judgment, he'd live an honest and straightforward life. Nope. The letter contained nude photos of the man. The envelope also had a letter saying that he "really really" liked her and hoped she wouldn't be upset with the revealing photos. She was. After her faced flushed with embar-rassment, it flushed with anger, and she sentenced the candid criminal to fourteen months in prison. Prison is a dangerous place for a man who likes to remove his clothes and take pic-tures of himself–but we'll see what develops.

YOU'RE ONLY PARANOID IF NO ONE'S REALLY WATCHING YOU

*T*wo young Wichita men had just dropped off their buddy in the parking lot of a liquor store and watched as he jogged inside to make a purchase. The two men noticed a parked police cruiser at the convenience store next door and became paranoid–they just knew the police were watching their every action. Although they hadn't done anything and had no reason to believe they were being watched, one of the men freaked out. He pulled a handgun from his pocket and, in the course of hiding it under the seat, accidentally discharged the weapon. The bullet went through his leg, through the front seat, and struck the man in the driver's seat. That's when the police arrived, right? Nope. The police were on a stakeout at the convenience market and were paying no attention to the dunderheaded drama at the liquor store–they didn't even hear the shot. What ultimately got the officers' attention, however, was when one of the men fell out of the parked car, limped a few steps, and threw something over the fence. The lame lame-o then got back into the car and sped away. The police pulled them over a few blocks later and helped get the two wounded occupants to a local hospital. I've heard of a victimless crime before–but a crimeless victim?

ARE YOU READY TO RUMBLE?!

A Columbus, Ohio, criminal thought he'd found the perfect person to rob–heck, he wouldn't even have to wear a mask. The would-be robber had targeted a blind man, thinking he would be an easy mark. The robber knew only one thing about his victim–he knew he was blind. He didn't know one other thing about the victim– he was a state wrestling champion. When the robber tried to strong-arm his victim, he found himself flipping through the air, slamming roughly into the ground, and being held in a half nelson until the police arrived. This is a good example of a criminal wrestling with whether to commit a crime or not.

In Dothan, Alabama, a wanted bank robber who had successfully eluded the police was finally captured when he was apprehended committing another crime—shoplifting an eighty-nine-cent carton of orange juice.

SIBLING RIVALRY

A man in West Haven, Connecticut, was arrested for
burglary when he attempted to gain access to a convenience store through the chimney—and became stuck.
There have been dozens of stories of stupid criminals
who have become stuck in chimneys, air-conditioning
ducts, grease traps, and the like, so what makes this story
unique? Well, a few years earlier the wedged thief's
brother had also been charged with burglary and had had
to be rescued—after he'd gotten stuck in the ceiling of the
same store.

RIGHT BACK AT YA

*T*he manager of the First American Bank in Annandale, Virginia, had just opened the front doors for the beginning of another business day and didn't notice the two men wearing bandannas, with pistols in their hands, rushing up behind him. Little did our two bandanna bandits know that the doors would automatically lock behind the manager. But they soon found out when the first robber hit the door at top speed and bounced back. He slammed into his partner, who was still running toward the door, and the force of the impact threw the first robber into the glass door once more. After they both picked themselves off the ground, they decided against attacking the door again and stumbled back to their getaway van. The van sputtered and stalled but finally turned over. The two bruised bad guys were able to escape undetected.

A DIFFERENT KIND OF CELL PHONE

An inmate serving time in a Genoa, Italy, jail escaped during a work program and left without a trace. Well, not exactly without a trace. The fleeing felon accidentally dropped his wallet while on the run, and the police confiscated it. Inside the wallet was the criminal's cellular-telephone number. Acting on a hunch (a hunch that the escaped prisoner was stupid), the police called the number and told the escapee he could pick up his lost wallet at police headquarters. Several hours later, the convict arrived at the station on a stolen moped to collect the wallet. Instead he was collected by the police and charged with evading jail and theft. It seems the man's cell phone had a clear signal, but his connection with reality was busy.

*A man in custodial care in a halfway house
was sentenced to one to five years in prison
for attempting to escape. The man had
decided to flee the confines of the halfway house
even though his sentence was set to expire
the following day.*

NINETY-PROOF MORON

*B*efore the cashier knew what was happening, a man with a shotgun appeared at the counter and demanded all the cash in the register. The cashier quickly filled a paper bag with the register's contents and handed it over to the shotgun-wielding robber. Before he made his escape, the robber saw a bottle of Scotch on the shelf behind the counter–and it looked pretty good to him. He stuck the barrel of the gun in the clerk's face and told him to put the Scotch in the bag with the cash. The cashier said he wouldn't do it. It wasn't that it was a particularly aged or valuable bottle of Scotch, he told the robber; he simply didn't think the man was old enough to drink. The robber claimed he was, but the cashier still refused to give him the liquor. To prove he was over twenty-one, the robber produced a valid driver's license and showed it to the conscientious clerk. The clerk looked it over, realized that the man was over twenty-one, and gave him the bottle of Scotch. The robber then dashed out of the store, ready to celebrate his newly acquired cash with a shot or two of fine single-malt Scotch. The cashier celebrated the man's stupidity by calling the police and giving them the robber's name and address, which he had memorized from the driver's license. The door to the thief's prison cell closed before he could even open his bottle of Scotch.

SIZE ISN'T EVERYTHING

A man drove into the small town of Brookshire, Texas, near Houston, and approached some locals, asking for their help. The man, who was a wanted criminal from Maryland, tried to sell them his spare tire in exchange for enough gas money to get out of town. The locals told the stranded stranger about the police chief's loan program, which was funded by local churches. The fund helps people get back on their feet and on their way home. Free funds sounded good to this felon; plus, he figured, the town was so small that its police certainly wouldn't have the ability to check for his name on the national crime-information computer system. The man walked into the police chief's office, explained his dilemma, and asked for some financial assistance. The man got his wish . . . sort of. He was able to get out of town all right, but it was because he was extradited back to Maryland when the chief, of course, ran his name through the system. Small-town police officers might, like Barney Fife, keep their bullets in their pockets, but they always keep their fingers on the computer keyboard.

WAIT UNTIL YOUR FATHER GETS HOME

A forty-one-year-old man robbed a Race Trac gas station in Cobb County, Georgia, and was quickly apprehended. He entered the store and used as his disguise (if you can call it that) a piece of cloth that covered only a portion of his face. The man must not have kept up with his daughter's work schedule, because she was the clerk on duty when he robbed the store. She reported him to the police, and he was arrested. In this case, Father doesn't know best.

A man was arrested while trying to break into a police car in Frome, England. Being that the windows were misted up, the man hadn't noticed the two policemen sitting inside the car.

THE CALL OF THE WILD

A burglar had quietly broken into a baker's shop in Villach, Austria, completely unaware that he was being watched. He was looking around the shop with a flashlight, trying to locate the safe, when suddenly he was attacked–by Lola the cockatoo. Caught completely off guard, the robber flailed about and accidentally knocked over a glass tank, setting free Egor, a viper. While trying to fight off the enraged cockatoo, who had become entangled in his hair, the robber watched in horror as the snake slowly slithered toward him. Enjoying the whole show from the safety of his cage was Peppino, the shop owner's pet mynah bird. Not wanting to be left out of the action, Peppino blurted out his favorite imitation–that of a doorbell ringing. The burglar decided to make a run for it and ran right through the shop's front window. When the store's owner came down to see what all the commotion was about, he saw his escaped pets and the escape route the burglar had taken. He also noticed blood around the window frame, as well as small pieces of the burglar's clothing left on the glass–the two thousand schillings in his safe, however, had been untouched. I've heard of a smash-and-grab thief before, but not a grab-and-smash.

WE'RE ALL IN THIS TOGETHER

An eyewitness spotted a man stealing a $1,400 gold chain from another patron at the Mall of America in Bloomington, Minnesota, and alerted the security guards. The security guards and the local police apprehended the man, and he was arrested. During the questioning of the witness, a background check revealed that he had several outstanding warrants against him, so he was arrested. Then the victim, the man whose necklace had been stolen, turned out to be in possession of crack cocaine, and he, too, was arrested. Three down, millions to go.

A man who intended to rob a post office burst through the doors of the wrong building and exclaimed, "This is a holdup!" The man was immediately arrested, as he had accidentally barged through the doors of the police station next door.

NOT HANDICAPPED ACCESSIBLE

A man quietly entered a Pompano Beach, Florida, bank and made his way to a teller's window. Holding up a brown paper bag, which he claimed contained dynamite, the man threatened to blow up the bank if he didn't get $900,000 immediately. Two customers and eight bank employees took the threat seriously and were able to sneak out the front door. Two other employees locked themselves in an office as the robber locked the front door to the bank. On the scene within minutes was Pompano Beach Police acting chief Larry deFuria, who began mediating with the robber through the thick glass window. The robber upped the ante; he now demanded a helicopter and "a million trillion dollars." It was then that deFuria knew he had to take action. He ordered one of his men to break the glass, and quick as lightning, deFuria burst into the bank and subdued the robber. Okay, more like tipped him over. You see, the robber was missing one eye and part of one leg, and was confined to a wheelchair—which the officer tipped over to catch the robber. The contents of the bag revealed not a bomb but a toothbrush, toothpaste, one cigarette, matches, pills, and paper. Police officers immediately recognized the robber because only minutes before he'd been at police headquarters, across the street from the bank, having just been released on trespassing charges. For a guy in a wheelchair, he sure did get around.

TRUE CONFESSIONS

*A*ndy Warhol said that everyone will get fifteen minutes of fame . . . and one La Grange, Illinois, burglar traded his fifteen minutes for a possible fifteen years. Merrill Shepro, who claimed to have robbed hundreds of homes during his career, appeared on *The Oprah Winfrey Show* in a segment about home security. During the show, Shepro, to prove that he might be a burglar but he certainly wasn't a liar, returned a set of rare, antique volumes of Shakespeare to a woman in the audience whose home he had burglarized. He might have thought of himself as a burglar with a heart of gold, but he had a head full of air. The police videotaped the show and took the tape to the grand jury as an on-air confession to burglary, and he was indicted. Maybe Ms. Winfrey should consider changing her Oprah Book Club to the Oprah Crook Club.

The police arrested a man in Youngstown, Ohio, after he took a walk on the wild side and stole six concrete sidewalk slabs from the corner of Forest Avenue and Shehy Street.

KEEPING IT IN THE FAMILY

A purse snatcher was arrested in Bari, Italy, after he chose the wrong person as his victim. The man, who was suspected of a string of handbag robberies, sped past his last victim on his motorcycle and deftly lifted her purse without slowing down. As he turned around to see the surprise on his victim's face, he realized he had made a relatively stupid mistake—the woman was his own mother. She immediately reported the incident to the police and said that she believed her son was stealing purses to finance his drug habit. The next time the mother and son were reunited, it was in a courtroom.

TOO MUCH TIME ON THEIR HANDS— MORE ZANY, WACKY PRISONER LAWSUITS

- Shortly after being made a jail trusty, inmate Ross Chadwell tried to escape the Benton County, Arkansas, Prison. He was soon captured and punished for his actions. He then filed a lawsuit against both the county and Sheriff Andy Lee, claiming civil rights violations. Chadwell accused Sheriff Lee of acting "recklessly" by making him a trusty and therefore putting him in a position that made it possible for him to attempt escape.

- Amil Dinsio, a federal prisoner in Loretto, Pennsylvania, filed a $15 million lawsuit against the United Carolina Bank in Charlotte, North Carolina. Dinsio, who'd robbed the bank in 1992, had been sentenced according to the amount of money he'd stolen. In his suit, Dinsio claimed that the bank had exaggerated the amount, which added sixteen months to his sentence.

- Merrill Chamberlain, who is serving a life sentence for the shooting death of an Albuquerque, New Mexico, police officer, had his lawsuit dismissed by the U.S. Court of Appeals in Denver. Chamberlain claimed that the police officer wouldn't have died if the officer had been wearing a bulletproof vest.

A NEARLY CATASTROPHIC THEFT

*I*t was a typically cold day in Moscow, and a man was on his daily walk with his pet Siamese cat. In order to speed up the walk and to help insulate himself against the frigid weather, the man decided to drape the cat across the back of his neck. A thief spotted the man walking alone and ran up behind him, reached out his hand, and grabbed the cat—thinking it was an expensive fur collar. The cat, not wanting his peaceful walk interrupted, sank his fangs and claws deep into the criminal's hand and arm. The attempted mugger ran off without a trace and must have gone home to lick his wounds. The local newspaper reported the incident, writing, "There is no animal more frightening than a cat, especially on its master's shoulders." This guy went from almost being a mugger to almost being a cat burglar.

ROCKS IN HER HEAD

A woman called the police, incensed because she believed someone had ripped her off. When an officer asked her what the substandard merchandise was, she said that it was two rocks. Was she talking about diamonds? Nope. She was talking about two rocks of crack cocaine. A police officer was dispatched to the woman's residence, where the woman angrily showed him the fifty-dollar rocks of cocaine and complained that they tasted like baking soda. The officer ran a field test on the rocks, they registered as being real cocaine, and he arrested the incensed (or senseless) woman on the spot. "It's amazing," said Assistant Police Chief Jerry Potts. "We've had people call and try to report robberies over dope, but we've never had someone call and say they got ripped off on a dope deal, and then we checked the cocaine and it actually was cocaine."

BLIND AS A FOX

*A*uthorities searched the home of a former U.S. Forest Service employee and uncovered truckloads of stolen merchandise, including ready-to-eat meals, tent straps, conference-room furniture, and a five-thousand-watt generator. But the man explained that he had an impairment that rendered him innocent of the charges. Did he claim kleptomania, multiple-personality disorder, amnesia, the heartbreak of psoriasis? Nope. The man claimed he was too blind to realize he had actually stolen that much stuff. His written excuse to Judge William Polly stated, "During the years of working for the Forest Service, I was conditioned to think it was customary practice to borrow and take excess government items. Due to my visual impairment, I didn't realize I had so many items on my property to be returned." Polly, however, could see right through the man's poor-eyesight excuse. "The evidence is absolutely overwhelming that he stole many, many things which far exceeded any mistake or oversight," Polly said. "He greatly abused the job and trust that was placed in him." Which prompts a question: Was the man out of sight or out of mind?

A LOFTY LIFTER

A man was seen shoplifting in a small store in Cookstown, Northern Ireland, and was immediately identified. The thief had stolen shoes, socks, and boxer shorts and was quickly and easily apprehended by the police. Even if he had worn a disguise, he would have been readily spotted–at seven foot five, the man was reported to be the tallest man in Ireland. Remarked one officer, "Everyone knows him, and you can see him coming a mile away." Of course everyone makes a mistake now and then–but this was a giant one.

The driver of a white Mazda was arrested in
Redondo Beach, California, and charged with
drunken driving. The police noticed the car
being driven erratically down the Pacific Coast
Highway, but what really caught their eye was
the upper half of a traffic-light pole lying across
the car's hood. When pulled over by the police,
the man's explanation of the pole was,
"It came with the car when I bought it."

KILL YOUR TELEVISION

I don't see why a man can't shoot his own TV if he
wants to," said Indianapolis loading-dock worker
Bobby Johnson. Johnson was arrested for criminal reck-
lessness after he emptied six bullets into his $900 Zenith
television set. The angered Johnson told the *Indianapolis
Star* that he'd capped the TV because his forty-one-
channel cable-TV provider offered him "nothing to
watch." And they say Elvis is dead!

LETTING THE CAT OUT OF THE BAG

A woman in Antioch, California, walked into a local police station and asked if they could run a test on some merchandise she thought might have been tampered with. Much to the surprise of the officer on duty, the woman produced a bag filled with methamphetamine. She was concerned that her boyfriend might have mixed in some hallucinogens. The next trip the woman took wasn't drug-induced; it was police-induced.

Trying to make a clean sweep, a man in Calgary, Alberta, robbed a Bank of Nova Scotia armed only with a bottle of household cleaner.

FEET, DO YOUR DUTY

*I*t was a spontaneous decision to break into a residential home in Oslo, Norway, and the burglar hadn't thought of everything–actually, he hadn't thought of anything. He entered the house without incident and quickly unhooked and removed two television sets, a videotape player, and some stereo equipment before he remembered that he was on foot and had no way of getting the stolen swag back to his apartment. He'd worked hard to pile up all that stuff and didn't want to just leave it, so our clever criminal called a cab. He stacked all the merchandise on the curb, sat down next to it, and waited for the cab to arrive. When the cab pulled up, the driver helped the man load all the equipment into the trunk and backseat; then the thief jumped in and gave the driver his address. Thinking it a bit odd that a man would be lugging around all that electronic equipment, the suspicious cabbie called the cops, who arrived at the thief's house and arrested him. Seems our clever thief should have thought about stealing a car first.

THIS PLACE IS JUST A HOLE IN THE WALL

A forty-one-year-old Helsinki, Finland, man was in desperate need of a pint of beer and decided to stop in at a local shop to bend his elbow. The fact that the shop was closed was of little consequence to our boozy burglar. He found a small window and broke out the glass–but not all the glass. As he tried to wedge his bulk through the opening, it became painfully obvious to his clouded brain that he wasn't going to get in . . . or get out. The man was stuck in the window, and the shards of glass that he hadn't knocked out were cutting into his stomach. According to the daily newspaper *Iltalehti*, the man, who was by now bleeding profusely and a little more sober, was discovered by the police and cut free of the window. He went from one hole in the wall to another.

Two robbers of a Pennsylvania bank were arrested because they failed to wear masks and were identified from tapes made by the bank's surveillance cameras. For some reason the two robbers thought that their faces would somehow be blurred if they smeared them with citric acid.

IS YOUR REFRIGERATOR RUNNING?

According to a story in the *New Orleans Times-Picayune,* an employee at the Edwards Elementary School stole one of the school's refrigerators and took it home. To her dismay, however, she discovered that the refrigerator wasn't working, so she called a repairman to fix it–but not any repairman; she called the school system's maintenance department. The repairman told the woman that he knew the refrigerator had been stolen from the school. The woman did not offer the man hush money to keep the refrigerator a secret–in fact, she didn't even offer him money for fixing the fridge. She must have thought that the school system should have been responsible for making sure their equipment was running properly–at least before someone stole it.

A FIRST-CLASP ROBBERY

A thirty-four-year-old Raleigh, North Carolina, man was arrested and charged with armed robbery after stealing a man's wallet at a local gas station. The victim was taken by surprise when the criminal thrust a cold, steel object into his ribs. According to the *Raleigh News & Observer,* the robber was armed with a regular office stapler. The police didn't know if the Swingliner was loaded or not; and if it was, whether the chamber was filled with standard staples or the deadly three-quarter-inch ones.

Two burglars were arrested and charged after breaking into and entering a house in São Paulo, Brazil. The burglar inside the house was unable to hear the warning of his friend on the outside, and the lookout didn't have strength enough to escape by himself—the burglars were both seventy-eight years old.

MINTY-FRESH THEFT

A man in West Haven, Connecticut, was browsing through the candy aisle at a local convenience store and eventually settled on a pack of gum as a treat. He took the gum to the counter and pulled out a dollar bill to pay for it. As the clerk was ringing up the purchase, the man brandished a gun and demanded all the money in the register. The robber grabbed the loot and made a clean getaway with the money and the gum. A few minutes later, however, he must have had an attack of conscience, as he reentered the store and asked the clerk, "Did I pay for the gum?" During the time between when the thief left and when he came back, the clerk had alerted the police, and they easily apprehended the criminal. Four out of five dentists would agree–this guy was an idiot.

I'M IN IT FOR THE MONEY

A suspect in a fourteen-year-old double murder finally came forward and surrendered himself to the police. Did the man's conscience finally get the better of him? Was he ready to make amends and seek forgiveness for his crimes? Nope. He wanted to collect the $3,000 reward that had been offered for his capture. The police rewarded him all right—with an all-expenses-paid trip to jail. "We believe he was serious about the reward. He will not be eligible," said Sheriff Lawrence Crow, Jr. And now he won't be eligible for anything, including parole, for a long, long time.

Quick Turnaround:

A prisoner in Buenos Aires, Argentina, who was released after serving fourteen years for murder, was arrested only seven minutes after he left prison—having gone only two hundred yards. He was charged with possession of stolen property he had obtained while behind bars.

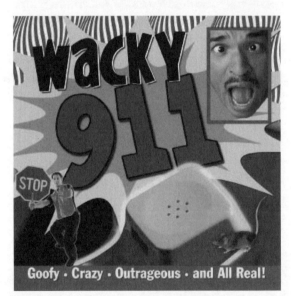